HE *Still* WALKS ON WATER

Copyright © 2024 by Gary J. Lewis

Published by Arrows & Stones and Pathway Press & Resources

All rights reserved. No portion of this book may be reproduced, stored in a retrieval system, or transmitted in any form or by any means—electronic, mechanical, photocopy, recording, scanning, or other—except for brief quotations in critical reviews or articles, without prior written permission of the author.

Unless otherwise noted, all Scripture quotations are taken from the New King James Version®. Copyright © 1982 by Thomas Nelson. Used by permission. All rights reserved. | Scripture quotations marked ESV are from The ESV® Bible (The Holy Bible, English Standard Version®), copyright © 2001 by Crossway, a publishing ministry of Good News Publishers. Used by permission. All rights reserved. | Scripture quotations marked GW are taken from the GW® Bible (God's Word Translation), copyright © 1995, 2003, 2013, 2014, 2019, 2020 by God's Word to the Nations Mission Society. All rights reserved. | Scripture quotations marked KJV are taken from the King James Version of the Bible. Public domain. | Scripture quotations marked MSG are taken from THE MESSAGE, copyright © 1993, 1994, 1995, 1996, 2000, 2001, 2002 by Eugene H. Peterson. Used by permission of NavPress. All rights reserved. Represented by Tyndale House Publishers, Inc. | Scripture quotations marked NASB 1995 are taken from the (NASB1995®) New American Standard Bible 1995®, Copyright © 1960, 1971, 1977, 1995 by The Lockman Foundation. Used by permission. All rights reserved. www.lockman.org | Scripture quotations marked NIV are taken from the Holy Bible, New International Version®, NIV®. Copyright © 1973, 1978, 1984, 2011 by Biblica, Inc.™ Used by permission of Zondervan. All rights reserved worldwide. www.zondervan.com. The "NIV" and "New International Version" are trademarks registered in the United States Patent and Trademark Office by Biblica, Inc.™ | Scripture quotations marked NLT are taken from the Holy Bible, New Living Translation, copyright © 1996, 2004, 2015 by Tyndale House Foundation. Used by permission of Tyndale House Publishers, Inc., Carol Stream, Illinois 60188. All rights reserved. | Scripture quotations marked TLB are taken from The Living Bible copyright © 1971 by Tyndale House Foundation. Used by permission of Tyndale House Publishers Inc., Carol Stream, Illinois 60188.

All rights reserved.

For foreign and subsidiary rights, contact the author.

Cover design by Sara Young
Cover photo by Max Reyes

ISBN: 978-1-962401-98-2   1 2 3 4 5 6 7 8 9 10

Printed in the United States of America

HE *Still* WALKS *ON* WATER

Gary J. Lewis

ARROWS & STONES

Pathway
PRESS & RESOURCES

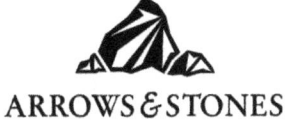

I dedicate this book to my wife, Lori: you are the love of my life—my soulmate, friend, advisor, prayer partner, and a steady voice on life's stormy seas. You never left my side as I traveled the long road of recovery following my accident. Your determination is only matched by your faith, love, and kind heart. You are an encourager, faith builder, and prayer warrior. I am thankful to God for bringing us together. I can't imagine walking this path with anyone else. I love you.

CONTENTS

Acknowledgments ix

Introduction 11

CHAPTER 1. Riding Into the Storm 15

CHAPTER 2. From Mountain to Valley 31

CHAPTER 3. Get in the Boat. 47

CHAPTER 4. Our Intercessor 63

CHAPTER 5. God, Where Are You? 79

CHAPTER 6. Going for a Walk 95

CHAPTER 7. Light in the Darkness. 109

CHAPTER 8. What's It Like to Sink? 121

CHAPTER 9. When God's in the Boat 135

CHAPTER 10. Here Comes the Son 149

CHAPTER 11. Oh, Come Let Us Adore Him! 159

CHAPTER 12. There's a Miracle Waiting!. 171

ACKNOWLEDGMENTS

Thank you to our three kids: Jordan, Jaren, and Sara. You put your lives on hold for months to take turns staying with us and helping your mother and me during my recovery. I love and appreciate you.

Dad and Mom, thank you; your love has always been an anchor in my life. You never wavered in believing that God would bring me through my storm. I love you.

I am grateful for our church family in South Georgia. To the state office team, you never missed a beat. Your strength and commitment were an encouragement to me. I couldn't have made it through without you. To the pastors and churches, you covered us in love, prayer, and support. I am better because of all of you. I love and appreciate you.

Thank you, Ride 4 Missions team (I think). You motivated me to start cycling, and our annual trek across South Georgia is always a highlight of the year for me. Your determination and encouragement gave me the courage to return to the bike and ride again.

Cindy Hall, thank you for the hours of reading and rereading the manuscript. Your input helped bring clarity to the message.

Finally, I am thankful to be a part of the global Church of God (Cleveland) family. Within minutes of my accident, prayers started going up before the throne room. Over the next several weeks of my recovery, numerous calls, texts, emails, messages, and posts of encouragement on social media came in from around the world. The church sent flowers and food. A pastor from Michigan even bought me a new bike (much to Lori's chagrin). You adopted me into your family as a young teenager (I was thirteen when I joined the Bethalto Church of God in Bethalto, Illinois). I met Lori (a fourth-generation COG member) at a Church of God school, East Coast Bible College. My children were raised in church parsonages and played on Church of God campgrounds. I love my church and will be forever grateful to be a part of the Church of God.

INTRODUCTION

Vision. It's the critical element, the drive, the burning passion within that catapults us to new heights, helps us cast aside setbacks, and keeps us moving regardless of the obstacles we face. It's the quality that moves us towards a goal we once could only imagine becoming a reality. As Hebrews 11:1 puts it, "Now faith is the substance of things hoped for, the evidence of things not seen." I think the word *vision* fits hand-in-glove with *faith*. Without these twin qualities at work in our lives, little gets done.

Vision led me to lace up my riding shoes on that Saturday morning in May of 2021 as I trained for our annual "Ride 4 Missions." Starting in 2018, each November, a group of two to three dozen volunteers trek nearly three hundred miles over three days from Dothan, Alabama, to Jekyll Island, one of four barrier islands along the coast of Georgia. All the money raised by bicycling participants (more than $200,000 in five years) goes to help support global missions. The 2021 project was the Berea Theological University in Zambia. Each rider has a passion for missions and this project specifically. The money collected through pledges raised by each cyclist goes towards training pastors and teachers from across Africa—who then return to their countries to minister to others' physical, material, and spiritual needs with the love of Jesus.

The reality of missions takes on a deeper dimension when considering what this college does: train pastors, educators, and church leaders to take the gospel across a continent of nearly 1.5 billion people. Roughly 40 percent of them are under the age of fifteen (compared to a 25 percent average worldwide), meaning some 560 million African children and teens need to hear the gospel. Ride 4 Missions helps build the theological school's dormitories and classrooms, equip ministers, and make youth seminars, church retreats, and marriage conferences possible. Steadily building a nation's moral fiber, instilling the truth in young people, and keeping families intact does more to strengthen a nation than millions of dollars in economic aid.

I set out to train for the latest ride on a typical late May day in South Georgia, with temperatures in the mid-eighties. The sun was shining, the birds were singing, and the magnolias were in full bloom. With a holiday weekend upon us, I got ready that morning in an optimistic frame of mind. I checked the air in my tires to ensure I wouldn't walk part of the way home, filled my water bottles, and donned my helmet, ready to ride.

As a runner, the one thing I will say in favor of bicycles is that they can transport you further and faster than possible on foot. I set out this day to ride twenty-six miles, just a fraction short of the distance of a marathon. Since I've run nearly ninety marathons, I knew I would have been straining a bit when I reached mile marker twenty-three. But this day, I inhaled a healthy gulp of fresh air and smiled as I thought, "Only three miles to home. I've ridden twenty-three miles and have only seen two cars. This has been a pretty good day."

The next thing I remember was waking up in a stranger's pickup truck.

"Where am I?" I asked, glancing at the road rash running down the side of my right leg and blood splashed down my body. "What happened?"

Chapter 1

RIDING INTO THE STORM

"When you pass through the waters, I will be with you; and through the rivers, they shall not overwhelm you; when you walk through fire you shall not be burned, and the flame shall not consume you."

—Isaiah 43:2 (ESV)

Across the United States, 966 bicyclists died in crashes with motor vehicles the year of my accident, a slight increase over the 948 fatalities recorded during the pandemic season of 2020.[1] Bicyclists in Georgia fared slightly better, with fifteen dying in 2021, compared to thirty-two a year earlier.[2] According to the Centers for Disease Control, more than 130,000 people are injured in crashes on US roads annually, with the costs of bicycle injuries and deaths from crashes exceeding $23 billion. Those figures include the expenses for health care and lost work

---
1 U.S. Department of Transportation, "Traffic Safety Facts 2021 Data: Bicyclists and Other Cyclists," *National Highway Traffic Safety Administration*, June 2023, https://crashstats.nhtsa.dot.gov/Api/Public/ViewPublication/813484.
2 "Traffic Data," *Georgia Governor's Office of Highway Safety*, accessed September 8, 2023, https://www.gahighwaysafety.org/traffic-data/.

productivity and estimates for lost quality of life and lives lost. About one-third of crashes resulting in a bicyclist's death involve alcohol use by the motor vehicle driver and/or the cyclist.[3]

In an overview of fatalities for 2021, the Insurance Institute for Highway Safety reported that although deaths had decreased 4 percent since 1975, they had increased 55 percent since reaching their lowest point in 2010: "Most bicyclist deaths in 2021 (90 percent) were among people age twenty and older. Deaths among bicyclists younger than twenty have declined 90 percent since 1975, while deaths among bicyclists twenty and older have quadrupled. In every year since 1975, many more male than female bicyclists were killed in crashes with motor vehicles. The decline since 1975 was far greater for females than for males (34 percent vs. less than 1 percent, respectively)."[4]

Of course, the day I wound up in the hospital feeling dazed with multiple injuries and tried to fathom what had just happened to me, such statistics were vague, meaningless minutiae. I didn't care about the national trend towards more bicycle paths and pedestrian safety, nor the push to increase mass transit usage so there are fewer vehicles on our highways. I was hurting. A careless driver—whether sober, impaired, or distracted by their cell phone—had smashed into me from behind, literally breaking my bike in half. I'm not sure how long I lay there, but I'm thankful somebody stopped to help. If he hadn't, I might have joined the 2021 fatality statistics.

After getting hit, I don't remember anything until I woke up in a pickup truck, wondering why empty cans and other trash

---

3 "Transportation Safety: Bicycle Safety," *Centers for Disease Control*, May 4, 2022, https://www.cdc.gov/transportationsafety/bicycle/index.html.
4 Highway Loss Data Institute (HLDI), "Fatality Facts 2021: Bicyclists," *Insurance Institute for Highway Safety*, May 2023, https://www.iihs.org/topics/fatality-statistics/detail/bicyclists.

were strewn around the floor. Since I didn't have my senses about me, I didn't know what was going on. When I asked what had happened, the driver replied, "You've been hit."

"Where are you taking me?" I asked.

"I was going to take you to the hospital."

"No, don't take me to the hospital," I said, shaking my head. "Just take me to my house. I live close to here."

Although I don't recall much from that morning, I remember asking, "Is my bike messed up?" and his answer: "Your rim was bent a little bit."

A little bit? My bike was broken in half, with the back smashed and part of it broken off from the frame! I thought my tire looked like a crushed aluminum ball.

Only about a mile from our house at that point, I directed him through several turns until he pulled into our driveway. The only reason I remember I had ridden in a pickup truck is the driver had thrown my bicycle in the truck's bed.

"If you remember where I got hit, I don't have my phone," I said.

"I'll get your phone for you," he said with a wave of one hand. "Don't worry about that."

After leaving my bike lying in the middle of my garage, he drove away. I never saw him again. He never retrieved my phone and never checked back to see how I had fared after the accident.

PICTURE OF PANIC

Of course, when I walked through the door with a torn shirt, road rash down my right side, and blood splattered across my body, my wife reacted as you might expect.

"We've got to go to the hospital right now!" Lori yelled. "I'm calling an ambulance!"

To add to the picture of complete shock, Lori didn't even know I had gone for an early-morning ride that Saturday. She had gotten up, headed downstairs to brew a cup of coffee, and started her morning with a devotion. Imagine a picture of a perfect Saturday morning, and the next thing you know, your husband is standing there bruised and bloody as he says, "I got hit by a car."

After her frantic reaction, I replied, "No, I don't need an ambulance." I just need to wash my face and get cleaned up. Lori guided me toward the car. Gesturing with my hand at the bike, I said, "Look at my bike. They destroyed my bike."

"I don't care about your bike!" she said, shaking her head. "Get in the car!"

In the spring of 2021, COVID-19 protocols were still in place, so when we reached the hospital, we had to first enter a tent in the parking lot for preliminary screening.

"If this was a hit-and-run, I've got to notify the police," the nurse said.

Suddenly, with the initial rush of adrenaline subsiding and every ounce of energy draining from my body, I interrupted the nurse to say: "I'm getting ready to pass out."

The woman quickly stood up and rolled her chair around the table for me to sit down. Orderlies quickly brought a gurney and placed a neck brace on me before wheeling me inside.

After doing an MRI, they brought me back to the emergency room (ER). Finally, a doctor came to the waiting area where I was resting. He told me I had suffered too much trauma for their small-town hospital to adequately treat my injuries.

"We're going to have to send you to the trauma center," he said, referring to a hospital just over a hundred miles to the north. "If it were just one thing, we might be able to deal with it here. I'm most concerned about your back being broken. I think you have a small puncture in your lung and might have a lacerated liver too." After listing a few other issues, he added, "I think it's too much for us."

I had to admit: I was a mess.

I had to admit: I was a mess. I had blacked out after getting hit so hard that it broke my helmet. For the next three weeks, I would periodically see little black dots dancing in front of my eyes. One of the doctors who treated me explained that head trauma builds up fluid behind the eyes, the source of those relentless dots.

GOOD SAMARITAN?

Before the drive to the trauma center, a police officer showed up to take my statement. After I related the whole story, he asked, "Do you think the guy who picked you up is the guy who hit you?"

"Probably," Lori interjected. "Because for one, why didn't he call 9-1-1? Common sense would dictate you don't move a body at the scene of an accident. If this guy had picked him up out of the goodness of his heart, he would have taken Gary to the hospital or stayed at the house to make sure he was okay, not just left the bike in the garage and drove off."

"We'll probably never find him," the officer said. "An isolated road like that and no witnesses or security cameras? Not likely."

In the months that followed, several friends asked if there were any security cameras in the area or at our house that might have captured an image of the motorist who ferried me home. But there weren't any. Whether the man had a warrant out for his arrest, was afraid we might sue him, or didn't have any insurance, we'll never know. But we are still thankful that he didn't leave me out there on that country road. I would never have made it those last three miles with my injuries and my bike destroyed.

FACING OBSTACLES

That discussion and my reaction are part of the hindsight of my accident. On that Saturday—just like that—I found myself in the turbulence and shear of a storm, not knowing what was going to happen next. The chaos broke my body, stirred up countless questions in my mind, and sent fear coursing through my veins. How will Lori manage? How will our children react when they find out what happened? The grandchildren? Will I need surgery? Am I going to recover? How much pain will I have to endure? Where was God in all this? Didn't He know that this was my first day of bike riding practice for the year as I prepared for the next Ride 4 Missions? Is this how my efforts to help His work get rewarded?

I don't know why bad things happen to God's people, or to anyone for that matter. But of this much, I am sure: sooner or later in life, we will all face obstacles. The toughest ones can look like trying to scale Mount Everest. We can find ourselves suddenly battling fear, guilt, and taunts from the devil, who is always trying to convince us that an all-knowing, all-seeing, all-loving God just doesn't love us. Satan may sneer, "God doesn't really care. If He did, would He have let this happen?"

I don't know why bad things happen to God's people, or to anyone for that matter. But of this much, I am sure: sooner or later in life, we will all face obstacles.

Vicious, nasty, dark clouds of despair can overwhelm us without a second's warning. That's exactly what happened to me on that pleasant Saturday morning when I had no idea I was about to ride into a storm that would change my life forever. As the cobwebs cleared from my mind once we reached the trauma center, it caused me to reflect on the suffering of Job on the day his children were enjoying a feast at their oldest brother's house. Then, like a tornado that swirls over the horizon, a succession of messengers bring the prophet the worst possible news about them:

The first told him an enemy had attacked, killed some servants, and made off with the oxen and donkeys.

The second said the fire of God had fallen from the heavens and burned up the sheep and other servants, and he alone had escaped to relay the news.

The third brought word that other enemies had formed three raiding parties to swoop down and steal the camels and put other servants to the sword.

Finally came the revelation that turned Job's stomach into a churning mess—while his sons and daughters were feasting and drinking wine, a mighty wind had swept in from the desert and struck the oldest brother's house. The four corners had collapsed and killed all of them, with only the messenger surviving to tell about the disaster (see Job 1:13–19 for full details).

One danger of casual Bible reading is missing the full picture of what happened to the characters in Scripture, regardless of the person. Sometimes, we treat Job's anguish with a shorthand version of reality. You know: "Poor Job, he lost some of his possessions and really had it hard." But let the details of that awful day sink deep into your spirit. Job had seven thousand sheep, three thousand camels, five hundred yoke of oxen, five hundred female donkeys, and numerous servants. Plus, his pride and joy: seven sons and three daughters. And *just like that*, he lost it all. Anyone who has suffered through the death of a single child knows the awful, sinking feeling of agony and dismay that overwhelms any parent. The kind that leaves them gasping for air and asking the universal question, "Why did this have to happen to me?"

Once you better understand the magnitude of Job's multiple losses, you may better appreciate his reaction to the parade of bad news messengers:

> *Then Job arose, tore his robe, and shaved his head; and he fell to the ground and worshiped. And he said: "Naked I came from my mother's womb, and naked shall I return there. The*

> LORD *gave, and the* LORD *has taken away; blessed be the name of the* LORD.*" In all this Job did not sin nor charge God with wrong.* —Job 1:20–22 *(emphasis added)*

Job didn't allow the storm to steal his hope. Every storm brings with it a spiritual battle, a clash where faith struggles to prevail over fear, and praise fights to drown out pain. Hope wrestles with helplessness. Love struggles to overcome loneliness. Only when we are equipped with vision and faith can we say as Paul did:

> *But thanks be to God, who gives us the victory through our Lord Jesus Christ. Therefore, my beloved brethren, be steadfast, immovable, always abounding in the work of the Lord, knowing that your labor is not in vain in the Lord.* —*1 Corinthians 15:57–58*

MORE SUFFERING

But Job's suffering doesn't end there. Chapter 2 describes Satan (and remember, God permitted Satan to do this) afflicting Job with painful sores "from the sole of his foot to the crown of his head" (v. 7). Imagine that: suffering so bad you sit with a shard of broken pottery and scrape yourself with it while sitting in an ash heap as your spouse tells you to curse God and die.

If that weren't bad enough, Job has to endure the insults of Eliphaz, Bildad, and Zophar, who essentially place Job under a microscope for the purpose of saying in effect, "What have you done wrong, buddy? Why have you sinned and brought this curse on yourself?" There's a reason similar second-guessers today carry the label: Job's Friends. And yet, after this series of charges and condemnations, Job is able to proclaim:

> *"For I know that my Redeemer lives, and He shall stand at last on the earth; and after my skin is destroyed, this I know, that in my flesh I shall see God, whom I shall see for myself, and my eyes shall behold, and not another. How my heart yearns within me!"* —Job 19:25–27

Not only was Job a wealthy man of faith, but he was also respected, generous, and known for helping the poor, widows, and orphans. Long before James wrote, "Pure and undefiled religion before God and the Father is this: to visit orphans and widows in their trouble, and to keep oneself unspotted from the world" (James 1:27), Job was doing just that.

In between the tragic news brought by the four messengers, the miserable comfort offered by Job's friends, and God finally answering Job's questions in a whirlwind, a number of qualities about this great man appear in chapter 29. As he writes in verses 7–12:

> *"When I went out to the gate by the city,*
> *When I took my seat in the open square,*
> *The young men saw me and hid,*
> *And the aged arose and stood;*
> *The princes refrained from talking,*
> *And put their hand on their mouth;*
> *The voice of nobles was hushed,*
> *And their tongue stuck to the roof of their mouth.*

> *When the ear heard, then it blessed me,*
> *And when the eye saw, then it approved me;*
> *Because I delivered the poor who cried out,*
> *The fatherless and the one who had no helper."*

In verses 13–17, he goes on to describe helping widows; wearing righteousness like a suit of clothes; striving for justice; helping the blind, lame, and needy; taking up the cause of strangers and intervening to help innocent victims from wicked people. In a commentary on Job, Dr. Art Lindsey—vice president of theological initiatives at the Institute for Faith, Work & Economics—writes:

> Job cared for the poor, the widow, and the orphan. He was an advocate for justice and righteousness. He must have helped many people. How many blind people would you have to help to call yourself "eyes to the blind"? How many lame people would you have to help to call yourself "feet to the lame"? Likewise, "father to the needy"?[5]

THE "WHY?" QUESTIONS

Still, alongside Job's words of faith emerged the struggle with the "Why?" questions. Why is all of this happening? What did I do? Where are you, God? In Job's book, he asks the Lord three specific questions:

1) Why was I born? (Job 3:11)
2) How can a man be just with God? (Job 9:2)
3) If a man dies, shall he live again? (Job 14:14)

---

[5] Dr. Art Lindsey, "Job: Putting the 'Righteous' in Righteous Rich," *Institute for Faith, Work & Economics*, 18 Jan. 2016, https://tifwe.org/job-righteous-rich/.

> *Pain pushes us to question, just as storms cause us to doubt.*

Pain pushes us to question, just as storms cause us to doubt. God answers Job's pleas and wonderings with a series of questions. Through them, He establishes His sovereignty. Regardless of the severity of the storm, God is still on the throne, and He holds us in His hand. Whenever we get to feeling, *Woe is me*, He is there to say things like:

> *"Where were you when I laid the foundations of the earth?*
> *Tell Me, if you have understanding.*
> *Who determined its measurements?*
> *Surely you know!*
> *Or who stretched the line upon it?*
> *To what were its foundations fastened?*
> *Or who laid its cornerstone,*
> *When the morning stars sang together,*
> *And all the sons of God shouted for joy?"*
> *"Or who shut in the sea with doors,*
> *When it burst forth and issued from the womb;*
> *When I made the clouds its garment,*
> *And thick darkness its swaddling band;*
> *When I fixed My limit for it,*
> *And set bars and doors; when I said,*
> *'This far you may come, but no farther,*
> *And here your proud waves must stop!'"* —Job 38:4–11

By this point, I would have been embarrassed as the Lord laid me out and "read my mail." God didn't stop there, either. His soliloquy goes on for another thirty verses in chapter 38 and all of 39 before pausing at the beginning of chapter 40 to ask, "Shall the one who contends with the Almighty correct Him? He who rebukes God, let him answer it" (v. 2). Small wonder that Job answered meekly, "Behold, I am vile; what shall I answer You? I lay my hand over my mouth. Once I have spoken, but I will not answer; yes, twice, but I will proceed no further" (vv. 4–5).

In response, the Bible describes the Lord speaking out of the storm:

> "Now prepare yourself like a man;
> I will question you, and you shall answer Me:
> "Would you indeed annul My judgment?
> Would you condemn Me that you may be justified?
> Have you an arm like God?
> Or can you thunder with a voice like His?
> Then adorn yourself with majesty and splendor,
> And array yourself with glory and beauty.
> Disperse the rage of your wrath;
> Look on everyone who is proud, and humble him.
> Look on everyone who is proud, and bring him low;
> Tread down the wicked in their place.
> Hide them in the dust together,
> Bind their faces in hidden darkness.
> Then I will also confess to you
> That your own right hand can save you." —vv. 7–14

Honestly, none of the Job lessons or insights came to mind as I lay there in the trauma center, shockwaves still periodically coursing through my body. It would only be later, as I reflected on this experience and what God wanted to teach me, that I developed a deeper appreciation for how Jesus can help us through any tough season of life, no matter what the loss, how crushing the defeat, or how paralyzed we might feel at the moment life takes a U-turn.

To grasp God's goodness, we must contemplate the full story of Job. Too often, we can get hung up on his losses but forget the end of this ancient saga. Sure, Job walked through unimaginable grief and suffering, but he also came out in better shape than before the storm hit. This is the part of Job's story worth remembering—that God is right there, walking through the storm by your side, whatever losses, grief, setbacks, or obstacles you are facing.

If you think of this as some kind of empty promise, consider the blessings God bestowed on Job at the end of the book:

> *Now the* LORD *blessed the latter days of Job more than his beginning; for he had fourteen thousand sheep, six thousand camels, one thousand yoke of oxen, and one thousand female donkeys. He also had seven sons and three daughters. . . .*
>
> *After this Job lived one hundred and forty years, and saw his children and grandchildren for four generations. So Job died, old and full of days. —Job 42:12–13; 16–17*

> *Jesus still walks on water. He still takes our hand and guides us through gut-wrenching, fear-inducing, nerve-rattling setbacks.*

The best news is that Job isn't some ancient figure whose relevance has faded with the passage of time. The same promises of restoration and blessing live on today through God's Son, the Savior Jesus Christ. Just like He did in the story described in Matthew 14:22–33, Jesus still walks on water. He still takes our hand and guides us through gut-wrenching, fear-inducing, nerve-rattling setbacks.

QUESTIONS FOR DISCUSSION

1) How has your life been affected by a sudden accident, death, or other tragedy? How did God help you through it?

2) Why do you think God allows tragedy to strike His children?

3) Did the material on Job in this chapter give you any new insights into Job's suffering? What about the blessings he received?

4) How has pain helped shape your life?

Chapter 2

FROM MOUNTAIN TO VALLEY

"So they all ate and were filled, and they took up twelve baskets full of the fragments that remained. Now those who had eaten were about five thousand men, besides women and children. Immediately Jesus made His disciples...."

—Matthew 14:20–22

Life is a series of mountaintops and valleys. We must be careful not to focus too much attention on either. Valleys can run so deep that we allow our struggles to overshadow our victories and good experiences. Likewise, we can't live on the mountain; God always has a purpose for our valleys.

I admire the song "God on the Mountain," written by famed gospel musician and pastor Tracy Dartt (who passed from this life in 2022). Recorded by over two hundred artists, "God on the Mountain" became a #1 hit song for The McKameys in 1988 and stayed at the top of the charts for five months. I love Dartt's lyrics reviewing how the God on the mountain is still God in the valley and how if He's God in the good times, He's the same in the bad times. As Dartt says, it's easy to talk about faith when we're up on the mountain, but in the valley of trials and temptations, our faith will face a test of its strength.[6] How true!

Whether on the mountain or in the valley, we can be grateful that we don't have to face life's ups and downs in isolation. The story of overcoming my accident is a huge praise to God who carried Lori and me through the storm—plus, the family, friends, ministry partners, and a church who walked through the storm with us.

Take what happened the day of my accident. Less than an hour after Lori called Mark Carver, our state church ministries director, and Justin Sharpe, our state youth director, to relay the news of my accident, they were in the ER, seeking to comfort her and ask if there was anything they could do. After learning the ambulance was going to transport me to the trauma center some two hours away, they told Lori, "We're not going to let you drive by yourself."

"I need to have my car," Lori said. "I don't know how long we'll be there, and I don't want to be stranded if I need anything or have to go anywhere."

"I will drive you," said Mark, while Justin added, "I will follow you, so you can come back."

Knowing both likely had preaching engagements the next day, Lori said, "That's too much to ask. We don't want to inconvenience you."

"No, we're not going to let you drive by yourself," Mark replied.

---

6   The Dartts, vocalists, "God on the Mountain" by Tracy Dartt, released 1995, track 3 on *Now*, Dartt Music Company.

Lori was glad they offered because on-the-road calls started pinging her phone immediately. But before answering those calls, she contacted our sons, Jordan and Jaren, and our daughter, Sara, my parents, and our siblings. Knowing how fast word can travel, she didn't want them to read about my accident on social media before they heard it from her first.

> *Life is a series of mountaintops and valleys. We must be careful not to focus too much attention on either.*

RECOVERY PROCESS

The afternoon I arrived at the trauma center, I looked like I had been run over by a truck, still wearing my shredded bicycle jersey and gravel clinging to my hair. I guess when they put the back strap on me at the hospital, they didn't want to move me again until I reached a more advanced treatment center. Because they couldn't find a bed for me until Sunday night, I lay in the ER for thirty-six hours. Finally, they wheeled me down the hall to take an MRI and find out more about my injuries.

They were primarily concerned with my back. When they first surveyed me at the hospital, the injuries doctors listed included a lacerated liver, a punctured lung, multiple broken ribs, a broken back, and head trauma, which included a nasty cut over my right eye. The doctor at the small hospital told me, "I don't feel comfortable trying to stitch your eye. I will apply a little butterfly stitch to hold you until you get there. That's one of their specialties, and they can handle it."

A butterfly stitch is an adhesive bandage commonly used to close minor, shallow wounds. They're an alternative to traditional needle and thread sutures and come in handy when customary bandages don't stick to moist body parts or move a lot. When I finally got settled in and the doctor saw me on rounds Monday, he removed the bandages and said, "I'm going to be honest with you. If we put butterfly stitches on, I think that wound will heal. I don't think you're going to need stitches."

> *I didn't need a single stitch on the cut across my eyelid. That began a miracle of healing that I can only attribute to God.*

I didn't need a single stitch. Today, I have a scar where it happened, but the only time someone can see it is when I close my eyes because the cut came down across my eyelid. That began a miracle of healing that I can only attribute to God. The trauma center was focused primarily on my back. Since they thought it was broken, they assigned my case to a neurosurgeon. On Tuesday, a doctor told me the lung would heal itself, so they didn't need to do anything. He said essentially the same about my liver; they would watch it to ensure nothing went awry. Nothing did.

All this offered confirmation of what the first ER doctor said to me before they sent me to the trauma center: "You're going to be okay. When I see people who are physically active and physically fit, their chances of recovery are leaps and bounds beyond folks who aren't fit, haven't taken care of themselves, and are on medication. I'm confident you're going to run again, and you're going to ride your bike again, so keep that in mind moving forward. You're going to be okay."

I took that as an affirmation the Lord would see me through the complex recovery process. I clung to that belief as I faced questions about what would happen, especially when I thought I might need surgery on my back.

GOD AT WORK

I saw more signs of God at work the day after I arrived. Lori's brother, David Barwick, skipped church so he and his wife could come to see me. When he got there, David talked about the numerous churches in our denomination they had passed along the way and how people in all those congregations were praying for me that morning.

"You're going to get through this," said David, not knowing how badly I needed to hear that message amid my pain. "It may not look like it right now, but God will get the glory, and you will be okay. The Lord's going to do a work in you."

Proverbs 16:24 says, "Kind words are like honey—sweet to the soul and healthy for the body" (NLT). Right then, David's words sank deep into my spirit, with the soothing effect that felt like he had administered a precious balm to my spirit.

More encouragement came from two of our pastor's daughters, Morgan and Jordan Dowd, who now lived in the area. Both had attended our youth camps when they were younger. Not only was one of them a nurse, but Morgan was also contracted to work at that hospital (a common phenomenon during the first part of the pandemic). She inquired why there was a long delay in securing me a room but couldn't find a definitive answer. When Lori called her Sunday morning, Morgan said, "I'll come after church to sit with Brother Gary, so you can come to my house and shower and rest a bit."

Physically exhausted and with her nerves frayed after a sleepless night in the ER, Lori greeted the offer joyfully. Of course, she was still concerned about me; she only slept for an hour before waking up and checking her texts. Seeing nothing about me, she called Morgan to ask if I was in a room yet. After learning I hadn't been moved, Lori sighed, "God, I don't know how I can handle another night in the ER."

She felt terrible for even feeling that way since I was the one with the broken back. But just as she was getting into her car to return to the hospital, Morgan texted: *They're putting him in a room right now.*

That wasn't the end of the day's blessings, either. When Lori called Jordan and Jaren, they wanted to come to the trauma center immediately, but she convinced them to wait until she knew more.

"We're not even in a room yet, and I don't have a place to go once they have one for your father," she said. "If you come here, you won't be able to stay with me, and I'll have to find a place for you to stay, and I'll be worried about that."

Sara (our baby) would have none of that kind of talk. Lori knew she had classes the next day at Lee University and tried to persuade her to hold off from coming. Since Sara reflects the determination she inherited from me, she replied, "I'm coming."

After our daughter arrived, she called Lori to tell her she had found a hotel five minutes from the trauma center. Lori fielded that call in the hospital, where she had delivered some sippy-cup-type drinks that I could consume while lying flat on my back. My night nurse was from Africa, which I had visited on mission trips to the continent many times. After we all chatted, she assured Lori: "He'll be okay. We'll take good care of him." Even though Lori didn't want to leave me that night because I was unable to move or do anything for myself, the night nurse's words reassured her she could go. Lori didn't realize how exhausted she was after thirty-six-plus hours in the ER. The hotel room was a welcome respite. Lori called our sons to tell them their sister had come but could only be there for one day, so they came the next day since visitation rules were so stringent.

Another unexpected blessing was Max Reyes showing up. Before moving to Michigan, he had served with us in South Georgia. Even though he only had a few hours after flying in to check on me, he helped Sara get a new iPhone for me and set it up (I never saw my old cell phone after the accident). The phone was vital because it connected me to family and friends, and it had a positive impact on my recovery. Calls of encouragement, prayer, and love began to come immediately through the new phone.

AN IMMEDIATE OCCURRENCE

Here, I want to depart from the account of my accident and its aftermath to look at the first lesson God taught me during this time of testing in my life. It was a time when I faced an "immediately." All of us have faced them when a great battle follows a great victory. While we like to pretend otherwise, a valley is on the other side of the mountaintop. This is what the disciples experienced in Matthew 14, a stirring chapter of history that relates the tragedy of John the Baptist's beheading and two of Christ's greatest miracles: 1) the feeding of thousands of people in the wilderness and 2) His walking on water.

> *All of us have faced an "immediately" when a great battle follows a great victory. While we like to pretend otherwise, a valley is on the other side of the mountaintop.*

The "immediately" for the disciples came after one of the greatest miracles of Jesus's earthly ministry. The story begins with a great multitude gathering around Jesus, who was moved with compassion for the people and healed many of their sick. When evening came, the disciples came to Jesus, imploring Him to send the multitudes away so they could leave this deserted place and go into the villages to buy food.

Instead of agreeing, Jesus offers them the impossible task of giving the people something to eat. Imagine being one of the disciples, scratching your head and thinking, *What? Are you kidding? How are we supposed to feed thousands of people out here in the middle of nowhere when all we have is five loaves of bread and two fish?* Well, with God, as Matthew 19:26 says, "All things are possible."

Jesus showed that in a remarkable way:

> *He said, "Bring them here to Me." Then, He commanded the multitudes to sit down on the grass. And He took the five loaves and the two fish, and looking up to heaven, He blessed and broke and gave the loaves to the disciples, and the disciples gave to the multitudes. So they all ate and were filled, and they took up twelve baskets full of the remaining fragments. Now those who had eaten were about five thousand men, besides women and children. —Matthew 14:18–21*

For two thousand years, this incident has been commonly described as "the feeding of the five thousand." Chances are, it was more like the feeding of the fifteen thousand. Or twenty. Jesus had just finished feeding five thousand men *plus women and children*. With large families the norm in those days, the numbers were much greater. No matter the exact count, He fed a multitude with only five loaves and two fish. Verse 20 says after everyone ate and was full, the disciples gathered twelve baskets full of the remaining fragments.

The disciples participated in this great miracle, collecting the leftovers. Immediately, Jesus sets the disciples on course toward a coming storm, which shows us that it is not uncommon to walk off the mountaintop and into a valley. A valley where, as Tracy Dartt liked to sing, God is the same God as He was earlier.[7]

---
[7] The Dartts, "God on the Mountain."

ON THE MOUNTAINTOP

Before going out on the lake, where they would confront some of their greatest fears, the disciples experienced the thrill of figuratively standing on a mountaintop and watching Jesus miraculously provide food for thousands of people—and, in a place where there were no food or fruit stands, no drive-through lanes, no 24/7 fast-food alternatives. Miracles are supernatural, mind-bending, unexplainable events demonstrating our Savior's divinity and incredible power. They weren't ordinary, everyday occurrences but startling occurrences that set the world buzzing and made the religious ruling Pharisees mad enough to kill him—literally.

However, this was only one of many mountaintop experiences for the disciples. Another appears in Luke 9:28–36. It starts with Jesus taking Peter, John, and James up on a mountain to pray, about eight days after Jesus had prophesied that some would live to see the establishment of the kingdom of God. As Christ prayed, the appearance of His face was transformed, and His clothing turned to a dazzling white hue (another eye-popping miracle):

> *Suddenly, two men, Moses and Elijah, appeared and began talking with Jesus. They were glorious to see. And they were speaking about his exodus from this world, which was about to be fulfilled in Jerusalem. Peter and the others had fallen asleep. When they woke up, they saw Jesus' glory and the two men standing with him. As Moses and Elijah were starting to leave, Peter, not even knowing what he was saying, blurted out, "Master, it's wonderful for us to be*

here! Let's make three shelters as memorials—one for you, one for Moses, and one for Elijah." —vv. 30–33 (NLT)

While on that mountaintop, the three disciples witnessed Jesus in His heavenly glory. And their first response was to make the place a memorial and linger there, just as we do today. We don't just make memorials; we create special ceremonies and festivals with annual parades, carnivals, souvenirs, concession stands, and food trucks. But the mountaintop was never meant to be the destination. They are simply milestones in our walk of faith, not eternal observances where we fall in love with our memories of the past instead of marching ahead in our walk of faith.

Mountaintops are simply milestones in our walk of faith, not eternal observances where we fall in love with our memories of the past instead of marching ahead in our walk of faith.

We can see this through God interrupting Peter as He laid out his plan to turn this mountaintop into a memorial:

But even as he was saying this, a cloud overshadowed them, and terror gripped them as the cloud covered them. Then a voice from the cloud said, "This is my Son, my Chosen One. Listen to him."

> *When the voice finished, Jesus was there alone. They didn't tell anyone at that time what they had seen.* —vv. 34–36 (NLT)

God didn't just set aside Peter's plans to create a Miracles "R" Us franchise; in Mark's Gospel account, we read that Jesus led the disciples back down the mountain and warned them not to tell anyone what they had seen until the Son of Man had risen from the dead (see Mark 9:9).

DON'T LINGER AT THE TOP

Don't miss the crucial point: Jesus told them not to dwell on their mountaintop experience. They needed to leave to see something even greater. Namely, the Son of God *would rise from the dead* (and I don't think they appreciated the enormity of this prophecy until they saw it with their own eyes). He was telling them there were more mountaintops to come. Likewise, if we stay on our current mountaintop, we can miss out on the next one. When we make the mountaintop a memorial and stay there, we may miss the milestones and mountaintops ahead.

We can't make the mountaintop our destination. In the valley, there are people who are suffering. There are needs to be met and people who need Jesus. Immediately after Jesus and the three disciples return to the valley, they encounter the father of a demon-possessed boy coming to Jesus for help. If we want to experience Jesus's glory on the mountaintop, we must also be willing to follow Him into the sufferings of the valley.

Now, the mountaintop gives us a unique vantage point. There are three viewpoints we can only see from the top of a mountain:

1) We see the valley behind us that we have just come through. Seeing where He has brought us from gives us the faith to trust Him with where we're going.
2) We see the valleys ahead. We know there is a storm on the horizon. But we can also see that there are more mountaintops in front of us. There are blue skies and sunshine-filled days ahead.
3) The view from the mountaintop gives us a perspective from above the storm.

Consider David's triumph over Goliath:

As the Philistine moved closer to attack him, David ran quickly toward the battle line to meet him. Reaching into his bag and taking out a stone, he slung it and struck the Philistine on the forehead. The stone sank into his forehead, and he fell face down on the ground. So, David triumphed over the Philistine with a sling and a stone; without a sword in his hand, he struck down the Philistine and killed him. David ran and stood over him. He took hold of the Philistine's sword and drew it from the sheath. After he killed him, he cut off his head with the sword. When the Philistines saw their hero was dead, they turned and ran. —1 Samuel 17:48–51 (NIV)

God's mighty hand had given David the greatest of victories: slaying a powerful enemy who had cowed Israel's warriors into timid silence. He had killed the Philistine warrior and put his army to flight. The people even sang about his conquest in the streets:

> *When the men were returning home after David had killed the Philistine, the women came out from all the towns of Israel to meet King Saul with singing and dancing, with joyful songs and with timbrels and lyres. As they danced, they sang: "Saul has slain his thousands, and David his tens of thousands."* —1 Samuel 18:6–7 (NIV)

FROM VICTORY TO STRUGGLE

David had just defeated the Philistines and Goliath. God had given the giant into his hand. This marked a miraculous victory for a young shepherd boy, one so small in stature that everyone passed him up when the prophet Samuel traveled to Bethlehem to see whom God had chosen from Jesse's family to be Israel's next king. Seven sons passed before Samuel, and seven times the Lord rejected them:

> *But the Lord said to Samuel, "Do not look at his appearance or at his physical stature, because I have refused him. For the* Lord *does not see as man sees; for man looks at the outward appearance, but the Lord looks at the heart...."*
> *And Samuel said to Jesse, "Are all the young men here?" Then he said, "There remains yet the youngest, and there he is, keeping the sheep." And Samuel said to Jesse, "Send and bring him. For we will not sit down till he comes here." So, he sent and brought him in. Now he was ruddy, with bright eyes, and good-looking. And the Lord said, "Arise, anoint him; for this is the one!"* —1 Samuel 16:7, 11–12 *(emphasis added)*

While the people may have been singing praises to David, not everybody shared their joy. The next day, Saul went from celebrating David's victory to resenting it. This is highly ironic, given the description at the end of chapter 16 of Saul sending a messenger to Jesse, asking him to dispatch David, so the lad could become the king's armorbearer. In addition, when distressing spirits came over Saul, David would take a harp and strum it, refreshing Saul and causing the spirit to depart. The fact that Saul was filled with jealousy and anger for the very man who had helped him fits into this category: What have you done for me lately?

First Samuel 18:8–11 (NIV) describes Saul as angry, with the people's refrain greatly displeasing him:

> *"They have credited David with tens of thousands," he thought, "but me with only thousands. What more can he get but the kingdom?" And from that time on, Saul kept a close eye on David.*
> *The next day, an evil spirit from God came forcefully on Saul. He was prophesying in his house while David was playing the lyre, as he usually did. Saul had a spear in his hand, and he hurled it, saying to himself, "I'll pin David to the wall." But David eluded him twice.*

This account shows how battles and struggles can follow miracles and victories. The victories prepare us for the battles, and the struggles prepare us for the miracles. Immediately after feeding thousands with just a few loaves and fish, the disciples headed into a storm.

God gives us the mountaintops to renew and refresh us, to take us from the trouble of the storm to the hope of the miraculous.

God gives us the mountaintops to renew and refresh us, to take us from the trouble of the storm to the hope of the miraculous. It strengthens our faith in the storm and lets us see the miracles ahead. We will miss the miracles and mountaintops in front of us if we stay on the mountain of our current victory.

QUESTIONS FOR DISCUSSION

1) How has a friend or loved one helped you in the midst of a setback? How did that draw you closer together?

2) What have you done to find relief in the midst of a major accident, illness, or setback?

3) How have you seen God provide for a need in a miraculous way?

4) Describe a mountaintop experience in your life. Why couldn't you stay there?

Chapter 3

GET IN THE BOAT

"Immediately, Jesus made His disciples get into the boat and go before Him to the other side, while He sent the multitudes away."

—Matthew 14:22

During my hospitalization and recovery, which included wearing a back brace for six months after I came home, I developed a deeper appreciation for Matthew 14:22–33. The story of Jesus coming to the disciples and nearly scaring them to death by walking on water is one of the most stirring in the Bible, with six lessons that apply to our daily lives:

1) When He says go, we must respond.
2) When He says give, we must open up our bank account.
3) When He says trust, we must cast aside all fear, doubt, and misgivings and (to use a familiar phrase) go "all in."
4) After pastoring three churches and serving in various church administrative roles for many years, I can assure you that our plans rarely match God's.

5) Faith demands looking beyond what sits in front of our eyes or exists in our rational, logical thought processes.
6) God's plans rarely make sense to human minds.

> *Difficulties don't necessarily mean we are out of the will of God any more than Job was when life plunged him into the midst of overwhelming grief.*

The lessons that stand out in the Matthew 14 passage start with the fact that God has a plan. In this story, we need to realize that the boat, the wind, and the waves were all a part of a grand design. The disciples were exactly where Jesus told them to be and doing what He told them to do. This is significant because it demonstrates that difficulties don't necessarily mean we are out of the will of God any more than Job was when life plunged him into the midst of overwhelming grief. A storm can be an integral part of the Lord's plan. So, while we may not like the idea of rowing into the midst of chaos and disaster, we have to get in the boat.

FACING THE STORM

That is what I saw as I lay in the trauma center for ten days, grappling with what had just happened but knowing that I had to trust Jesus to walk with me through this storm. In chapter 2, I mentioned how I never needed stitches across my right eye.

That was just the beginning of Jesus walking on water for me. The most startling episode of healing involved my back. As I understand it, the problem when you break your back is the compression in your spine. When it breaks, the rest of your back caves in on the broken, weakened area of the spine. This often requires doctors to go in and insert a rod to keep the rest of your spine from continuing to collapse. But after my MRI two days after the accident, the doctor came in and said, "I think it is an error with the X-ray: there's just a hairline of decompression. Instead of compressing, the X-rays we just took show a hairline going in the other direction. We're going to wait a day before we do anything. We'll take another one tomorrow and go from there. If there is no further compression, surgery may not be necessary."

When they took another X-ray on Tuesday, there was no further compression despite my burst and broken vertebrae. At this point, I was still flat on my back; I hadn't moved since Saturday when they took me to the trauma center. They had brought a back brace for me on Saturday, but the doctor wouldn't let them put it on then, saying it was too early. On Tuesday, when the doctor said, "We'll wait this week and see how it goes," I replied, "I'd love to get the back brace on today. I aim to walk a hundred steps down the hallway and sit in that chair for about an hour."

"Those sound like good goals," said the doctor, who agreed to my request.

"I'm going to do this," I declared. From that point on, I set my focus on getting better. Wednesday, Thursday, Friday, Saturday

…each day, I would walk further down the hallway and progress toward my objective of getting better.

Now, before this, I had never been in the hospital. Never. No broken fingers, wrists, or legs like so many kids suffer in playground accidents or from falling out of a swing in their backyard—no severe case of the flu, either. None of our children had ever needed to be rushed to the ER, had their tonsils out, or suffered an illness that required anything more than a quick visit to our primary care doctor. I had never taken a single prescription medication either. The first night when that doctor had come in, he said, "We've got these muscle relaxers, oxycodone, and other pain relievers."

I had broken ribs, and while I knew my back was broken, it didn't hurt if I stayed still. So, I said, "I think I can get by with just some Tylenol."

"You're not going to be able to just get by on Tylenol," the doctor said. "But I'll give you some, and during the night, you can ring your buzzer, and the nurse will bring you something stronger."

I don't know what they gave me in the ER shortly after I arrived at our local hospital. Most of that day was a blur, and since they were giving me all the medications through my IV bag, I assume they probably gave me some kind of pain medication initially. But from that first night in the trauma center, I never took anything more substantial than a Tylenol.

PAINFUL OBEDIENCE

As you know by now, I never saw this storm coming. But when it did, I vowed not to allow the waves to swamp me and render me helpless. I got in the boat and trusted God to keep me moving forward. As for the disciples, several of them were seasoned fishermen and likely recognized the signs of a coming storm. They probably didn't understand why Jesus would send them into a pending disaster. But faith outlasted fear, and obedience overcame doubt, so they got into the boat and launched into the sea.

Obedience to the Lord isn't always easy and can often be uncomfortable. Sometimes, we don't understand the purpose of a valley or how it fits into God's plan for our life. There are times when we must (as 2 Corinthians 5:7 says) "walk by faith, not by sight." They require the belief to say, "God, I don't understand why I'm going through this storm. It doesn't make sense. But I choose to trust You!"

> *Obedience to the Lord isn't always easy and can often be uncomfortable. Sometimes, we don't understand the purpose of a valley or how it fits into God's plan for our life.*

Scripture shares a story familiar to many about three young Hebrew men. Like the disciples, they chose obedience in the face of uncertainty. Shadrach, Meshach, and Abednego demonstrate the power of faith in the fire. The Daniel 3:8–29 story starts with a group of astrologers who came forward to denounce the Jews. I sense all kinds of petty jealousy and envy in their actions.

Babylonian astrology represented the first such known system, and by the time Daniel's top aides arrived, it had been around for several centuries. The Babylonians were a polytheistic people who believed in many gods. They charted the seasonal movement of the sun, moon, and planets as part of their beliefs in determining their gods' divine intervention in daily life. Now, here were these Hebrew intruders, claiming to follow the one true God and threatening everything the astrologers held dear. Here was an opportunity to put these intruders in their place.

To advance their cause, these soothsayers used a time-tested tool: flattery. Praising King Nebuchadnezzar and saying he should live forever, they reminded him he had issued a decree that whenever folks heard the sound of things like a horn, flute, or harp, and all kinds of music, they were to fall down and worship the image of gold.

To say the image was intimidating would be an understatement. This statue stood ninety feet tall, equal to a nine-story building, and measured nine feet wide. Whoever didn't worship this king's creation would be tossed into a fiery furnace. Yet here were several Jews Nebuchadnezzar had set over the affairs of the province who were ignoring the decree. The astrologers complained that they neither served the king's gods nor worshiped the gold image he had created.

HEATED ANGER

Naturally, as the astrologers knew he would, the king grew furious over this apparent challenge to his unquestioned authority. So, Nebuchadnezzar summoned the three key advisors. You can imagine the king seething when he asked if it were true that Shadrach, Meshach, and Abednego weren't serving his gods or worshiping the image of gold. Like often happens in such situations, powerful people always offer underlings an escape hatch: if the trio would bow down and worship the image when they heard a horn or other instruments and music, all would be forgiven. But if they refused, they would face immediate punishment in a furnace blazing with fire. If they did, the king doubted any god would be able to rescue them from his all-powerful hand.

The three Jews made him madder with their reply that they didn't need to defend themselves; throw them into a blazing furnace, and the God they served would deliver them from it, as well as the Babylonian majesty's hand. But even if that didn't happen, they wanted Nebuchadnezzar to know that they wouldn't serve his gods or worship the gold image.

Not only was he furious, but his attitude ramped up several notches; Nebuchadnezzar ordered his minions to stoke the furnace, so it was seven times hotter. No wonder the flames killed the soldiers who took Shadrach, Meshach, and Abednego and threw them into the blazing furnace. Now, between Daniel 3:23 and 24, there may have been some brief interlude that Daniel didn't describe. I say that because the action immediately switches from the three men getting tossed into the furnace to King Nebuchadnezzar leaping to his feet in amazement and asking if they had thrown three men into the fire because he saw four men walking around, unbound and unharmed, and the fourth looked like "a son of the gods" (v. 25, NIV).

That's when the king approached the opening of the blazing furnace and called to the men to come out. I think it's pretty interesting he used the expression "servants of the Most High God" when he did. Scripture says:

> *Then Shadrach, Meshach, and Abed-Nego came from the midst of the fire. And the satraps, administrators, governors, and the king's counselors gathered together, and they saw these men on whose bodies the fire had no power; the hair of their head was not singed nor were their garments affected, and the smell of fire was not on them. Nebuchadnezzar spoke, saying, "Blessed be the God of Shadrach, Meshach, and Abed-Nego, who sent His Angel and delivered His servants who trusted in Him, and they have frustrated the king's word, and yielded their bodies, that they should not serve nor worship any god except their own God! Therefore, I make a decree that any people, nation, or language that speaks anything amiss against the God of Shadrach, Meshach, and Abed-Nego shall be cut in pieces, and their houses shall be made an ash heap; because there is* no other God who can deliver like this.*"—vv. 26–29 (emphasis added)*

PATH TO TROUBLE

With God, the path we follow may lead through a fiery furnace, a stormy sea, or a mangled bicycle. It may be uncomfortable and even disagreeable, but whatever is going on, remember that God always has a purpose for what we are going through. Lori saw that when she went through the aftermath of my accident and how it helped grow her faith.

"I've always felt I trusted God, and, in this situation, there was nothing else I could do but trust Him with my husband, our lives, and our ministry," she said, reflecting recently on this experience. "I didn't know what life would look like after this accident, but I didn't dwell on that. I just thanked God that Gary was alive and that He had kept him."

> *With God, the path we follow may lead through a fiery furnace, a stormy sea, or a mangled bicycle.*

In other words, Lori had an experience similar to that of Lazarus and his sisters, Mary and Martha. When He raised Lazarus from the dead, Jesus used it to reveal that God's purpose works everything for our good, whether seen or unseen. This reality reflects the truth of Romans 8:28: "And we know that all things work together for good to those who love God, to those who are the called according to His purpose."

Many of you reading these words know the story from John 11 and how Lazarus fell ill. That prompted his sisters, Mary (who earlier had anointed Jesus with expensive, fragrant oil and wiped His feet with her hair) and Martha, to send word to the Lord that the one He loved was sick.

> *When Jesus heard that, He said, "This sickness is not unto death, but for the glory of God, that the Son of God may be glorified through it." Now, Jesus loved Martha and her sister and Lazarus. So when He heard*

that he was sick, He stayed two more days *in the place where He was.* —vv. 4–6 *(emphasis added)*

I must pause here to observe that Jesus didn't react by dropping everything and dashing off to Bethany. Today, most people would consider Him rude or unfeeling, even insensitive to the predicament of close friends. What did Jesus have in mind, lingering where He was so things could get worse? A greater work than healing Lazarus. Namely, His friend's resurrection: "Then Jesus said to them plainly, 'Lazarus is dead. And I am glad for your sakes that I was not there, that you may believe'" (vv. 14–15).

Through the lens of this storm, Jesus revealed the power of God's purpose for His people.

No one understood it; everyone questioned it, and some even resisted. But God had a plan! That's why Jesus first pointed out: "This sickness is not unto death but for the glory of God." Regardless of the origin or cause of a storm, in it and through it, all glory belongs to God.

Heartache, sickness, and distress are inevitable in this world. In 2 Corinthians 6, Paul emphasized that we are workers together with Christ and equipped to persevere by His grace. No matter our circumstances or vocational calling, we are called to "commend ourselves as ministers of God" (v. 4) without getting offended but demonstrating patience and enduring distasteful things like tribulation, sleeplessness, and imprisonment. The sustenance of the Lord during adversity gives us a testimony and witness to the power of Christ.

STORMS ARE POSITIVE

Next, Jesus revealed the uncomfortable yet powerful truth that God uses storms for our good. It is difficult to see and comprehend since the pain and suffering associated with our storms can keep us from seeing God's plan. Jesus was teaching His disciples that supernatural faith is forged in fire. The faith that would become the rock upon which the church would be built (and still stands) was perfected through storms. This brings to mind Psalm 46, especially verse 10: "Be still, and know that I am God; I will be exalted among the nations, I will be exalted in the earth!"

I've already mentioned that as a result of my accident, my back was broken in three places. I suffered a punctured lung, broken ribs, lacerated liver, and head trauma. And when I arrived at the trauma center on that fateful Saturday, I immediately began to see the hand of God at work in my storm. There were still many moments of doubt, fear, and faithlessness ahead, but on this day, I chose to trust His plan even when I couldn't see it or understand it. I did not know how my story would end, but God did. He had it all under control and was busy working it all out.

I may not understand, and I may not know why, but I know in whom I have believed, and I'm going to trust His heart and hand to see me through.

We will never know true victory as a believer until the issue of God's sovereignty is settled. After all, He is God, and we are not! There will be things we don't understand and can't figure out or agree with. But whether we understand it or not, God has a plan. I may not understand, and I may not know why, but I know in whom I have believed, and I'm going to trust His heart and hand to see me through.

Numerous Scriptures apply to this point:

- "Many are the plans in the mind of a man, but it is *the purpose of the Lord* that will stand" (Proverbs 19:21, ESV, emphasis added).
- "For *I know the plans I have for you*, declares the Lord, plans for welfare and not for evil, to give you a future and a hope" (Jeremiah 29:11, ESV, emphasis added).
- "Before I formed you in the womb *I knew you*, and before you were born *I consecrated you*; *I appointed you* a prophet to the nations" (Jeremiah 1:5, ESV, emphasis added).

How do we trust God's plan when we don't know what it is? When we go through a trial and ask ourselves, What happened? I thought God had such great plans for me, but all I see is hardship! Well, our job isn't to fit all the pieces together. It's simply to follow God's lead as He fits all the pieces together. Proverbs 3:5–6 says, "Trust in the Lord with all your heart, and lean not on your own understanding; in all your ways acknowledge Him, and He shall direct your paths."

WAITING ON GOD

Waiting is never easy. It's hard to trust when you don't know what's happening. However, there are four very practical things you can do when God's plan or purpose isn't clear:

1) Remember that God is all-powerful.

God can do anything. He created the entire universe, from the tiniest speck to vast oceans, with nothing more than the sound of His voice. It does not matter how impossible your situation seems to you. It's never too big for God. Never. It's why He told the prophet Jeremiah, "I am the LORD, the God of all mankind. Is anything too hard for me?" (Jeremiah 32:27, NIV). And why Luke wrote, "For with God nothing will be impossible" (Luke 1:37).

2) Remember that God cares for us.

We often don't question whether or not God *can* do great things but whether or not He *will*. We reason that it doesn't benefit us if God can come through for us but chooses not to; in such cases, we fail to realize our problem is that we think because God has delayed giving us an answer, He will never provide one.

3) Don't lose sight of the big picture.

Just because God loves you and wants what's best for you doesn't mean you will always enjoy sailing across a calm, smooth lake. In the middle of a trial, consider the big picture. Your circumstances may not be your preference, but God isn't just concerned with your happiness. His plan is much larger and more comprehensive. Sometimes, the painful circumstances we endure now are what we need to prepare for the amazing things God has in store for us later.

4) Practice being patient.

Sometimes, waiting on God comes down to being patient. We're not going to get everything we want, and everything doesn't always work out our way. That doesn't mean God doesn't care or He's not in control. Too many people's prayers for patience could be phrased, "I want patience, Lord, and I want it right now!" Don't engage in making such an illogical request. Patience (also called longsuffering in some translations) is one of the nine fruits of the Holy Spirit listed in Galatians 5:22–23. We must recognize that our wisdom, vocational skills, or talents don't produce this fruit. The Spirit produces patience in us as we live with His power and trust Him to guide us through life.

QUESTIONS FOR DISCUSSION

1) Have you ever had (or have now) a physical obstacle like Gary's back brace that hindered your movement? How did you overcome that?

2) After reading this chapter, do you have a greater appreciation for how the Lord has a plan for setbacks in our lives? Why?

3) Do you find it hard sometimes to trust that God has a plan for your adversity? Why?

4) How can you develop more patience?

Chapter 4

OUR INTERCESSOR

"And when He had sent the multitudes away, He went up on the mountain by Himself to pray."

—Matthew 14:23 (emphasis added)

During my ten days in the trauma center, I prayed regularly. However, I didn't lie there in agony, pleading, "God, help me." I was more focused on what I had to do to get better and would ask the Lord for His help to move forward. I asked that He help me recover quickly so I could return to my ministry and tend to my responsibilities. I asked Him to help Lori navigate the worries and emotional upheaval that every spouse feels when the person closest to them faces a threat to their life or wellbeing. I asked Him to give our children peace, comfort, and the knowledge that their dad would be all right. I asked Him to help staff members at the office to carry on in my absence. I asked Him to remind me that so much of what I see in my daily life as urgent isn't really all that urgent in light of a life-changing catastrophe.

> *I would love to say I kept calm throughout this crisis, but that wouldn't be true. Still, during these times of prayer and reflection, God gave me a peace that is hard to explain.*

I would love to say I kept calm throughout this crisis, but that wouldn't be true. Still, during these times of prayer and reflection, God gave me a peace that is hard to explain. It was a real-life example of what Paul wrote to the Philippians: "Be anxious for nothing, but in everything by prayer and supplication, with thanksgiving, let your requests be made known to God; and the peace of God, which *surpasses all understanding*, will guard your hearts and minds through Christ Jesus" (Philippians 4:6–7, emphasis added).

People who have been around church for many years can treat Paul's pledge like a cliché. But it is very real, as sound and solid as the chair I am sitting on as I type these words. Because of God's peace, I believed everything would be all right. The Lord helped me walk through the valley at the trauma center and the following valleys. This sounds like such a traumatic experience (and on one level, it certainly was) that recently, someone asked me if I suffered any symptoms of PTSD—post-traumatic stress disorder. Not really. It may sound like I should have, but I didn't. Again, not because I'm some spiritual giant, but because I serve a Jesus who is always interceding for us. In the story outlined in

Matthew 14, He went up on the mountain by Himself to pray, and according to Hebrews 7, He is still doing that.

The passage from Hebrews 7:24–27 (emphasis added) is so powerful it is worth repeating it here:

> *But He, because He continues forever, has an unchangeable priesthood. Therefore, He is also able to save to the uttermost those who come to God through Him since* He always lives to make intercession for them. *For such a High Priest was fitting for us, who is holy, harmless, undefiled, separate from sinners, and has become higher than the heavens; who does not need daily, as those high priests, to offer up sacrifices, first for His own sins and then for the people's, for this He did once for all when He offered up Himself.*

LASER-FOCUSED

With the story of Matthew 14, we must keep a central thought in mind: Jesus never lost sight of the disciples. He could see them from His place of prayer on the mountainside. The description of this incident in Mark's gospel (Mark 6:45–56) adds this critical detail to the Matthew 14 account: "*He saw the disciples* straining at the oars because the wind was against them" (Mark 6:48, NIV, emphasis added).

Wow! While the disciples were fighting harsh waves amid the storm, Jesus was interceding for them. We have an intercessor who is always on the job. In this case, His prayer for the disciples wasn't for the storm to cease but that they summon the courage to face reality and not lose their faith.

After all, He controls the wind and waves, which is evident in Luke's description of the time the disciples crossed a lake with Jesus:

And a windstorm came down on the lake, and they were filling with water and were in jeopardy. And they came to Him and awoke Him, saying, Master, Master, we are perishing! Then He arose and rebuked the wind and the raging of the water. And they ceased, and there was a calm. But He said to them, "Where is your faith?" And they were afraid and marveled, saying to one another, "Who can this be? For He commands even the winds and water, and they obey Him!" —Luke 8:23–25

Jesus constantly prayed for His disciples despite their weak faith and other shortcomings. Mark 6:51–52 says of the rescue on the Sea of Galilee: "Then he climbed into the boat with them, and the wind died down. They were completely amazed, for they had not understood about the loaves; *their hearts were hardened*" (NIV, emphasis added). Jesus was interceding for their souls, reflecting the truth outlined by the prophet Isaiah: "'For my thoughts are not your thoughts, neither are your ways my ways,' declares the Lord. 'As the heavens are higher than the earth, so are my ways higher than your ways and my thoughts than your thoughts'" (Isaiah 55:8–9, NIV). So often, we focus on the external storm when His focus is on helping us with our internal storm. He is our omniscient, omnipotent intercessor.

I'm grateful for the intercessors that God has placed in my life. . . . I know they were hard at work while I was lying flat on my back in the trauma center.

I'm grateful for the intercessors that God has placed in my life. Those wonderful saints who continually bring my name to the throne of God and prayer partners who hold up my hands in times of battle or fatigue. I know they were hard at work while I was lying flat on my back in the trauma center. Numerous people assured me of that in the cards, letters, emails, and other messages that came through Lori before my release and directly to me after I went home.

THE VALUE OF INTERCESSORS

My in-laws, Wallace and Mary Barwick are another sterling example of intercessors. Before their deaths in 2015 and 2016, they were known as prayer warriors to believers in their church. Unbelievers in their small town of Jesup, Georgia (population 9,900), recognized them as people who knew God and would pray for them in their times of need. Over the years, countless people showed up at their front door, asking for prayer. We endured difficult seasons, and they would wake up in the middle of the night to call out our names in prayer; those prayers helped sustain us. My parents, Arthur and Sadie Lewis, have prayed fervently for us and, during this recovery time, enlisted the prayers of their church as well. Phone calls, cards, and letters all reinforced their constant prayers on our behalf. My mother's sisters, Lucy Richardson and Lola Newell, have spent countless hours undergirding us in intercessory prayer throughout our ministry.

Lori's Uncle Walter and Aunt Mamie Alice (who has since passed) were prayer warriors God used in our lives. They were intercessors for our family and ministry from the beginning. It is difficult to place a value on prayer partners like them, who held up our hands and covered our hearts with intercessory prayer. They would often call so they could pray with us, knowing that ministry could be challenging for a young family.

As a pastor, Reverend Barwick understood the pressures and demands of ministry. They served our church as pastors and state leaders and offered direct and powerful prayers. In his nineties, Uncle Walter continues to pray for us daily.

There are countless others whom God has raised up in our ministry, like the intercessors at churches where we pastored. They consistently held up our arms and stood with us. For years, ministry partners and family members have called our names out before the throne of God. Such men and women have silently partnered with our ministry on their knees, standing with us in seasons of tragedy and triumph and sustaining us with their intercession.

As I was writing the words to this chapter, I received a text from such a prayer warrior, who wrote: *I'm praying that as you plow, sow, and water, the ground will bring forth a bountiful harvest for His kingdom. Knowing that others have joined you on your ministry journey is encouraging.*

A tangible sign of my intercessors' help could be seen two weeks after I came home from the hospital when I attended our state's summer camp meeting. This annual gathering brings together churches from across South Georgia. It's a highlight of the year for thousands of members—a time of worship, preaching, teaching, fellowship, and celebrating God's victories in our lives. Lori tried to persuade me not to go. Our children were against it, too. But I felt it was essential to be there and show by my presence that we serve a God greater than anything the world can throw at us.

I also wanted our church to know their prayers had been of enormous help in keeping my spirits up, maintaining my peace, and giving me the energy and determination to work through my recovery. The danger of reading a summary of what I overcame is thinking that it wasn't that tough and that I never wavered. I can assure you that I had the same struggles, doubts, and questions anyone else would have after such an accident.

THE POWER OF INTERCESSION

Attending that week of meetings took some grueling preparations. Just getting dressed was an ordeal. I had to wear a T-shirt under my back brace to prevent it from rubbing against my body and leaving sores. And wear clothing over the brace in an attempt to look as normal as possible. As you can imagine, moving around requires a lot of effort. But receiving all the greetings, prayers, and other encouragement that came my way was worth it. A friend of ours who took pictures during the meetings later showed me the difference: on the first day, I barely had my hands raised, but by the end of the week, they were high in the air. It was like God had performed a miracle in a few days. My being there meant a lot to numerous people; one woman told Lori afterward: "You don't know how much it meant to us to see him there."

Intercessors weren't just active during the weeks and months after my accident; they have been around throughout my ministry. Some were only with me for a season, while others have been praying for me from the beginning. Their impact on my ministry, family, and life is immeasurable. I'm thankful that God raises intercessors in our lives. They support our arms when we grow tired, just as Aaron and Hur did for Moses on the battlefield, and carry us until we can see the victory.

I'm thankful that God raises intercessors in our lives. They support our arms when we grow tired, just as Aaron and Hur did for Moses on the battlefield, and carry us until we can see the victory.

This is why the writer of Hebrews encourages: "Let us therefore come boldly to the throne of grace, that we may obtain mercy and find grace to help in time of need" (Hebrews 4:16). It's why Paul wrote, "Rejoice always, pray without ceasing, in everything give thanks; for this is the will of God in Christ Jesus for you" (1 Thessalonians 5:16–18). And why the apostle John could promise we can pray with confidence: "Now this is the confidence that we have in Him, that if we ask anything according to His will, He hears us. And if we know that He hears us, whatever we ask, we know that we have the petitions that we have asked of Him" (1 John 5:14–15).

Intercessory prayer is straightforward. It's asking God to do something in a person's life, church, or situation. It is coming to God on behalf of someone else. As Paul encouraged Timothy:

> *I urge, then, first of all, that* petitions, prayers, intercession, and thanksgiving be made for all people—*for kings and all those in authority, that we may live peaceful and quiet lives in all godliness and holiness.* —1 Timothy 2:1–2 (NIV, emphasis added)

In Luke 11:5–8, Jesus tells the parable of the friend who had been on a long trip and came to his friend's house at midnight. The traveler was very hungry, but his friend had no bread to give him. Being concerned for his hungry friend, the man went next door and pounded on the door so his neighbor would get up and give him some bread. But his neighbor didn't even come to the door, instead shouting (in effect), "Go away! I'm in bed, and my children are in bed. Come back in the morning!" Instead of giving up, the man kept pounding and shouting until his neighbor got up and gave him the bread he needed to feed his hungry friend.

This parable teaches us the power of persistence in prayer; we must pray and never give up. But the parable is also a perfect picture of intercession. There are three friends in this story: 1) one has a need and is hungry, 2) another friend can meet that need because he has the bread, 3) there is the friend in the middle who brings the two together by going to one on behalf of the other. It is the most selfless kind of prayer.

A NEEDY WORLD

This is where God has placed every one of us. We are surrounded by a world with needs, whether spiritual, emotional, or physical. Many have needs we cannot meet, but we know the One who can. And in prayer, we are called to go to God on behalf of those around us. We are called to be intercessors. It is a powerful ministry to pray for others and a blessing to see God work in their lives. There are some people whose main spiritual gift is intercession. Still, we are all called to be intercessors and to make a difference in the world through intercessory prayer.

We are called to be intercessors. It is a powerful ministry to pray for others and a blessing to see God work in their lives.

Paul's relationship with the Philippians is an example of intercession's power. We know that the Philippians loved Paul. When Paul wrote to them, he was in a Roman prison. The struggles that the Philippian church had watched Paul endure broke their hearts. Miles away, they had no political power to change his situation. But they knew the power of prayer, so they prayed to God, and their prayers changed everything. Paul wrote, "Yes, and I will rejoice, for I know that through your prayers and the help of the Spirit of Jesus Christ, this will turn out for my deliverance" (Philippians 1:18–19, ESV). God acted when his people interceded. This is still true today.

To intercede means "to intervene on behalf of another." We see this in many different places throughout the Bible. Moses interceded for the people of Israel, and we see the Philippians praying to God on behalf of Paul. God partners with His people to bring about His will. The Philippians partnered with God to bring about His will for the church in interceding for Paul; you and I get the same call today to partner with God in prayer.

Intercession does not mean manipulating God but instead seeking God's will for someone and praying for that will to be fulfilled. Paul knew that the Philippians were praying for God to help him. It is easy to become discouraged and frustrated in difficult storms, but we need to remember that God is good and desires good for His children. Psalm 100:5 says, "For the LORD is good; his steadfast love endures forever, and his faithfulness to all generations" (ESV). In 1 John 5:14, the apostle assures: "And this is the confidence that we have toward Him, that if we ask anything according to his will, he hears us" (ESV). Hebrews 4:16 encourages us to "come boldly to the throne of grace."

God will not give someone something they don't need or that isn't good for them just because they asked for it.

When praying to God's heart, we can come to Him confidently. We may not always feel like we approach God with confidence. We may pray for the wrong things. At times, we will because none of us can discern the will of God perfectly; however, we can trust God. He will not give someone something they don't need, or that isn't good for them just because they asked for it. Romans 8:26–27 tells us that when we don't pray for the right things or don't know what to pray, the Holy Spirit intercedes for us according to the will of God. And Romans 8:34 says that Jesus is interceding for us as well!

Scripture encourages us to pray. Consider also these verses:

- "We always thank God for all of you and *continually mention you in our prayers*" (1 Thessalonians 1:2, NIV, emphasis added).
- "For this reason, since the day we heard about you, *we have not stopped praying for you*. We continually ask God to fill you with the knowledge of his will through all the wisdom and understanding that the Spirit gives" (Colossians 1:9, NIV, emphasis added).
- "And pray in the Spirit on all occasions with all kinds of prayers and requests. With this in mind, be alert *and always keep on praying for all the Lord's people*" (Ephesians 6:18, NIV, emphasis added).

A GREATER ONE

The call of an intercessor is biblical. All believers are called to intercede for one another. We are instructed to pray without ceasing. Christians are to stand in the gap for all people, as

God invites us to participate in His work through intercession and prayer. These qualities are the primary ingredients to a victorious life.

However, there is One even greater! We have a heavenly intercessor: Jesus, our advocate with the Father in heaven. As our intercessor, Jesus knows our circumstances better than we do. We are limited by a finite view of life, seeing only what is here now. We only know what we can remember of what has been. But He has an infinite view. Jesus sees what was, what is, and what is to come. While He exchanged an altar made of boulders on a seaside mountain for a throne in glory, His role as intercessor has never ceased.

This assurance appears in numerous passages, starting with Hebrews 7:25, which says, "He always lives to make intercession." What a tremendous promise! Our risen Savior is alive and praying for us. He is standing in the gap, intervening and interceding. He has the heart of a shepherd watching over His sheep and the love of a bridegroom for His bride. This is why Paul could write to the church in Rome: "Who is he who condemns? It is Christ who died, and furthermore is also risen, who is even at the right hand of God, *who also makes intercession for us*" (Romans 8:34, emphasis added). Through the power of His sacrificial death and glorious resurrection, He intercedes for us.

Paul includes intercession on his list of priestly sacrifices Jesus makes for us: "And the Lord said, 'Simon, Simon! Indeed, Satan has asked for you, that he may sift you as wheat. But I have prayed for you, that your faith should not fail'" (Luke 22:31–32, emphasis added). Did you notice what happened here? Jesus prayed for Peter's faith to not fail. While our focus is on our sifting, His focus is on us standing. Jesus didn't pray for Peter to avoid the storm, He prayed for Peter's faith to sustain him through the storm.

> *While our focus is on our sifting, His focus is on us standing. Jesus didn't pray for Peter to avoid the storm, He prayed for Peter's faith to sustain him through the storm.*

This was the same kind of prayer Jesus offered in His legendary prayer on the eve of His crucifixion in John 17: "After Jesus said this, *he looked toward heaven and prayed*: 'Father, the hour has come. Glorify your Son, that your Son may glorify you'" (v. 1, NIV, emphasis added).

The cross lies before Jesus in the hour of His agony. As our priestly intercessor, we find Him praying. But this prayer was not just for the weary, sleepy disciples in the garden with Him, but for all who would follow:

> *"My prayer is not for them alone. I pray also for those who will believe in me through their message that all of them may be one, Father, just as you are in me, and I am in you. May they also be in us so that the world may believe that you have sent me. I have given them the glory that you gave me, that they may be one as we are one—I in them and you in me—so that they may be brought to complete unity. Then the world*

will know that you sent me and have loved them even as you have loved me." —vv. 20–23 *(NIV, emphasis added)*

This latter prayer for unity within the church would be so great that it would change the world. The prayer of a High Priest without sin, interceding for a sinful world, proclaimed the eternal love of the Father for His people. The priestly prayer of Jesus for His disciples, then and now, demonstrates the intercessor's heart He has for His children. His prayers continue to this day on behalf of His disciples.

The priestly prayer of Jesus for His disciples, then and now, demonstrates the intercessor's heart He has for His children.

As our heavenly intercessor, there are many reasons only Jesus can perfectly intercede on our behalf. He is fully God and fully man, yet without sin (see Hebrews 4:15). Jesus understands our struggles and temptations; Satan tempted Him in the wilderness, yet He did not sin (see Matthew 4:1–10). He lived a holy life and then paid the price for our sins through His death on the cross. Jesus is God's only Son. At His baptism, God the Father spoke, saying, "You are my beloved Son; with you, I am well pleased" (Luke 3:22, ESV). The Father's love shines forth in the familiar words of John 3:16–17:

> *For God so loved the world that He gave His only begotten Son, that whoever believes in Him should not perish but have everlasting life. For God did not send His Son into the world to condemn the world, but that the world through Him might be saved.*

Today, Jesus is in heaven, advocating on our behalf against the accusations of Satan. Jesus paid for our sins once and for all on the cross, taking on our sins so that we might take on His righteousness. We are now accepted as blameless before God and can boldly approach His throne because we have an intercessor who has made everything possible.

QUESTIONS FOR DISCUSSION

1) Have you ever felt the peace that passes all understanding described in Philippians 4:7? How did that change your life?

2) Have you ever thought of Jesus as your intercessor? What difference does that make?

3) Have you prayed regularly for your pastor or other church members? How has that affected you? How has it affected them?

4) What is one prayer you would like to see God answer today?

Chapter 5

GOD, WHERE ARE YOU?

> *"Now, in the fourth watch of the night Jesus went to them, walking on the sea."*
>
> —Matthew 14:25

When we're lying flat on our backs after getting run over, we can quickly wonder where God is—both when it happens and in the aftermath. I confess to such feelings after my crash when, in fact, God was already at work. Take the care and comfort extended to Lori during the crucial hours after my mishap.

In chapter 2, I told you about our state directors driving Lori to the trauma center two hours away at a time when she was barely able to cope with the shock of what had just happened. And how our daughter Sara made the two-hundred-mile drive from her campus to be with us. But there's more to the story. While I mentioned how Sara found a hotel five minutes from the hospital, I didn't share that many of our churches and ministers helped with the expense of their ten-day stay, along with meals and incidentals.

Our church has a tradition of caring for people in times of need, whether in South Georgia, where I was serving at the time, or across the wider church globally. It is easy to take such a thing for granted until we face a crisis because life has just given us a gut punch, leaving us reeling and wounded.

While we didn't see it as a blessing when it happened, Lori and I already knew what storms were like because of the tremendous damage inflicted by Hurricane Matthew in 2016, not long after we had moved to Georgia. While much of the total $16.5 billion losses came in Haiti and other areas of the Caribbean, nearly 1.5 million people in Florida, Georgia, and South Carolina lost power. They had weeks of clean-up to deal with after Matthew moved on. Although the worst damage occurred along the coast, Matthew inflicted torrential rains inland in several states that sparked widespread flooding.

Everyone has their own trials, tragedies, and losses to endure, which is why we must continually be aware of the faithfulness of God.

This was only the first of several hurricanes or tornadoes that would strike the region during our six years in Georgia. Sometimes, we wondered if catastrophe had followed us down the highway when we moved south from Tennessee. Everyone has their own trials, tragedies, and losses to endure, which is why we must continually be aware of the faithfulness of God. It never ceases to amaze me. He cares for us, teaches us in the midst of trauma, and prepares us for future storms.

ALWAYS ON TIME

We can miss the significance of that phrase in Matthew 14:25: "Fourth watch of the night." The fourth watch drew its name from the Roman practice of placing guards on a night watch at three-hour intervals, which had replaced Israel's traditional three watches of the day. So, the fourth watch referred to the hours of 3:00 a.m. to 6:00 a.m.

Ironically, while we may think of that as prime time for sleeping, some Christians see the early hours as the best time for communing with God. Biblically speaking, strategic things happened then. God called to Samuel four times in the middle of the night (1 Samuel 3:3–10), Jacob concluded his wrestling match with the angel at dawn (Genesis 32:22–31), Moses led Israel across the Red Sea in the dark (Exodus 14:26–27), and the angels appeared at night to announce the Savior's birth (Luke 2:8–14).

Baptist Pastor David R. Smith says the early hours can be a great time to encounter God: "'God hears us perfectly at all hours of the day. But we can't so easily dismiss him at 3 o'clock in the morning,' Smith says. 'He's okay with calling you out of a comfortable sleep. He doesn't operate on our time.'"[8]

As accurate as that is, if we were with the disciples and had been waiting all night and wondering how we would survive, we

---

8 Diana Aydin, "The Fourth Watch: Listening for God at Night," *Guideposts*, accessed October 10, 2023, https://guideposts.org/angels-and-miracles/miracles/gods-grace/the-fourth-watch-listening-for-god-at-night/.

could understand why the disciples felt exhausted and beaten on the Sea of Galilee. All hope seemed lost. The storm showed no sign of clearing. Jesus must have missed it. He was late. Or worse, had forgotten them.

However, the disciples were about to learn a life-altering truth: He is always on time, even when we think He's running late. Unfortunately, very rarely does my time coincide with God's time. Impatience causes me to question His timing. I love how singer, songwriter, and record producer Dottie Peoples puts it in her song "He's an on Time God." She sings about how while He may not come when you want, He will always be there on time.[9]

It may help you appreciate this tune more if you knew what led her to write it in 1994: She was traveling to a revival. Running late, Dottie grew anxious since she believed she would cause the program to start late. But the service hadn't started when she arrived, and people were waiting for her. As she walked on stage, she remembered that God's timing is perfect, no matter how late we may think He is.[10]

In other words, God is not held captive by our deadlines and schedules. His time is always the right time. We often prolong our difficulties because we struggle with God to get out of our storm rather than trusting Him to guide us through our storm. And there is a vast difference between getting out and getting through. Getting out says, "I don't want to learn or grow; I just want the pain to stop." Getting through says, "I don't understand

---

9 Dottie Peoples, vocalist, "He's an on Time God" by Dottie Peoples, August 30, 1994, track 3 on *Dottie Peoples and the People's Choice Chorale*, AIR Records & Tapes.
10 Jennifer Bell, "The Meaning Behind the Song," *Guideposts*, August 13, 2023, https://oldtimemusic.com/the-meaning-behind-the-song-on-time-god-by-dottie-peoples/.

it, and it doesn't make sense to me, but I'm going to hold to God's unchanging hand and trust Him to see me through."

We often prolong our difficulties because we struggle with God to get out of our storm rather than trusting Him to guide us through our storm.

After living through my 2021 bike accident, I can say that no one—especially me—enjoys trials and setbacks. Sometimes, it seems our difficulties and storms last longer than they should. We know there's got to be a shorter path or a quicker route to get us to the other side of the storm, but God chooses to take us a different way.

There have been times when He's kept me in a hard place longer than I wanted to stay. When divine detours kept me in a difficult place longer than expected, I found myself questioning God's plan. Yet I have also learned that His timing is different from ours. He sees the big picture; we see only a snippet. When He keeps us in a hard place instead of delivering us right away, it's so that we can grow to depend on Him more. As we do, we will see Him mold, shape, and conform us to His image. The storms teach us patience as they help strengthen our trust and faith. They help us to grow in spiritual maturity and become more sensitive to His calling on our lives. As Isaiah 40:31 says, "But they that wait upon the Lord shall renew their strength; they shall mount up with wings as eagles; they shall run, and not be weary; and they shall walk, and not faint" (KJV).

A CALL FOR PATIENCE

Though the storm may be fierce, and we grow faint and weary, He calls us to be patient and trust Him because He loves us and cares about us. This is why James said to "count it all joy when you fall into various trials, knowing that the testing of your faith produces patience. But let patience have its perfect work, that you may be perfect and complete, lacking nothing" (James 1:2–4).

We will often ask, "Why?" and agonize over when it will all end. Just as the disciples wondered what was happening during their storm, we can rarely see the significance of one or why it must happen. Yet we must wait on God. As Isaiah 55:8–9 teaches, His ways are higher than our ways and His thoughts higher than our thoughts. We don't always know the reason behind how God works in our lives or why He chooses a particular storm for one person, family, or group, and not another. We will never have all the answers. We simply need to learn to trust Him.

No matter how long the storm lasts or how hard the trial, He is always working behind the scenes. Even when it seems like nothing's happening (or especially when it seems like that). He has not forgotten us or left us. Even when it doesn't feel good, when it hurts, He is working it out for our good.

When I was walking through the process of my recovery, still uncertain where the road ahead would lead, I would recall the times in my life when God had delivered me from storms and difficulties. Meditating on the times when He was evident in my life and accomplished things that appeared impossible to man but were possible with God, strengthened my faith. You might say it took it to a whole other level.

Remembering those times encouraged me to continue trusting Him. After all, He had never failed me before. Likewise, we can't allow our storms to blind us to His faithfulness and diminish His promises for our lives. Our soul must rest in His promises. He brought us through the storm before and is faithful to bring us through the storm again. When we learn to trust His timing and purpose, we can have faith that He will be with us the whole way.

Recently, Lori and I were at a McDonald's drive-up window. It seemed like it was taking an eternity to get our food. Complaining about the slow service, I grumbled, "I could have gone inside and gotten it quicker."

"Calm down; it's only been a few minutes," my wise wife replied.

In my frustration, I added, "Honey, it's called 'drive through,' not 'sit through.' I didn't come to fellowship with these folks. I want to give *my* order, pay *my* money, pick up *my* food, and be on *my* way." (Sometimes the truth can be embarrassing.)

In our quest to escape life's difficulties, we can treat God that very same way. There is no time for growing or giving. Does God not realize how dire our situation is? We get tired of waiting for the answer. But God is not a fast-food restaurant employee whom we command at our whim, nor does He deliver when we expect it. He is the Creator of the universe. He is the King of Kings and Lord of Lords. He operates on His timetable, not ours.

Seeing what we perceive as a slow response can make us think God is not listening to us when in reality it is us not taking time to be patient. God is patient with us, and He wants us to be patient and trust Him. It is very easy to compare ourselves to others and wonder why He has come through *for them*, but it has yet to happen *for us*. We cannot forget that there is a purpose and reason for something not happening or not changing like we think it should. We should be like David when he wrote: "My times are in Your hand" (Psalm 31:15). And remember how God acted on Joshua's behalf: "And the sun stood still, and the moon stayed, until the people had avenged themselves upon their enemies.... So the sun stood still in the midst of heaven and hasted not to go down about a whole day" (Joshua 10:13, KJV).

HE'S NEVER LATE

It is impossible for God to be late. He holds time in His hand. Time does not dictate to God. He is omniscient and omnipresent and transcends space and time. We can grow impatient when our time doesn't coincide with His time. In chapter 3, I mentioned how Mary and Martha experienced the power of God's timing when their brother Lazarus was sick and then died. Divine delays can be perceived as divine distance. But He is always near, He always cares, and He is always on time.

Divine delays can be perceived as divine distance. But He is always near, He always cares, and He is always on time.

There's more to this story in John 11 than what I noted previously—how when Jesus heard Lazarus was sick, He waited two more days in the place where He was. In addition to that, when He said to the disciples, "Let us go to Judea again," the disciples acted with what today we might call righteous indignation: "Rabbi, lately the Jews sought to stone You, and are You going there again?" (v. 8).

Talk about walking into a storm! If the disciples were confused about Jesus leaving them to battle vicious waves on the Sea of Galilee, they were equally perplexed by the idea of the Lord returning to the scene of the crime, so to speak. Putting Himself in harm's way? Intentionally? How is that supposed to work? Well, remember what I mentioned earlier in this chapter about God's ways and thoughts being higher than ours?

Not only did they not understand Jesus wanting to go back to Judea where His enemies could take another run at Him, but they didn't understand His remark about Lazarus being asleep but going to wake Him up. Only when He explained that Lazarus was dead and that He was glad for the disciples' sake so that they would believe in His miraculous power, did they start to grasp what was happening.

It wasn't just the disciples who struggled to understand the storm of Lazarus dying (albeit temporarily). As soon as Martha heard that Jesus was coming, she went out to meet Him. We can hear the anguish in her voice and feel the waves of emotion rolling through her heartbroken soul as she says to Jesus, *"Lord, if You had been here, my brother would not have died.* But even now I know that whatever You ask of God, God will give You" (vv. 21–22, emphasis added).

Here I have to pause to acknowledge that Mary has the reputation of being the most devoted follower of Jesus while her sister gets tagged as the workaholic of the family. But in the passage we just looked at, Martha is making a ringing declaration of faith: "I know that whatever You ask of God, God will give you." Wow! That is a statement of strength and unwavering belief, the kind we need to summon when a storm is raging and we can't understand what is happening and why.

Not only did she believe that God the Father would grant anything Jesus asked of Him, but when Jesus tells her He is the resurrection and the life, and the means to eternal life for all who believe in Him, Martha responds: "Yes, Lord, I believe that You are the Christ, the Son of God, who is to come into the world" (v. 27). Trusting His timing brings revelation of His power. In the waiting, Martha saw the resurrection power of Jesus! The pain of delay was replaced by the power of faith. Through the pain her response was, "Yes, Lord, I believe…."

That's when Mary comes on the scene and falls down at the Lord's feet, repeating the anguished cry her sister had made: if You had been here, Lazarus wouldn't have died. Jesus's response is full of caring and compassion:

> *Therefore, when Jesus saw her weeping, and the Jews who came with her weeping, He groaned in the spirit and was troubled. And He said, "Where have you laid him? They said to Him, Lord, come and see." Jesus wept. Then the Jews said, "See how He loved him!"* —vv. 33–36 (emphasis added)

Trusting the Lord's timing brings a fuller revelation of His person. When Jesus saw her broken heart, He wept with her. In every season of waiting, there is revelation. We must choose to trust His hand and heart in our time of difficulty. God never promised us that our life on earth would be easy, but He did say that "there is a time for everything, and a season for every activity under the heavens" (Ecclesiastes 3:1, NIV).

Many things that we consider good end up countering with something we consider bad, but God has told us there is a purpose for it all. In Ecclesiastes 3, Solomon goes on to recount the many ways:

A time to be born and a time to die, a time to plant and a time to uproot, a time to kill and a time to heal, a time to tear down and a time to build, a time to weep and a time to laugh, a time to mourn and a time to dance, a time to scatter stones and a time to gather them, a time to embrace and a time to refrain from embracing, a time to search and a time to give up, a time to keep and a time to throw away, a time to tear and a time to mend, a time to be silent and a time to speak, a time to love and a time to hate, a time for war and a time for peace. —vv. 2–8 (NIV)

God always provides for us, and that provision always comes at just the right time—not a moment too late, and never too soon.

The point is this: He always provides for us, and that provision always comes at just the right time—not a moment too late, and never too soon. He rescues us at the right time, like He did David:

*I waited patiently for the L*ORD *to help me, and he turned to me and heard my cry. He lifted me out of the pit of despair, out of the mud and the mire. He set my feet on solid ground and steadied me as I walked along.* —Psalm 40:1–2 (NLT)

We may feel mired in tough circumstances that only seem to get worse. We cry to God for help and if a rescue doesn't appear immediately, panic sets in. But patience and panic can't share the same space in our hearts. The psalmist chose patience because he understood God's nature. He had a grasp on God's wisdom, sovereignty, and love that enabled him to trust God's timing. He knew God would respond, not a moment too soon or too late—but right on time. Our God is wise, sovereign, and loving. He hears our cries, and He comes at just the right time.

His will is not a roadmap. It's a relationship. It doesn't always work according to our calendar or clock. God has a greater purpose than just getting us from point A to point B. There will be many times in life when we don't understand God's timing. Naturally, given our human weakness and limited understanding, in such times it will be easy to become impatient and frustrated.

Unfortunately, when we don't understand God's timing, it may lead us to try to take action. As the old saying goes, "I'm going to take matters into my own hands!" But rash declarations and actions only lead to more problems. They may even compound the difficulties we are already facing. Exhibit A is Abraham and Sarah, trying to speed up God's promise of a child, as outlined in Genesis 15–21.

Abraham was seventy-five years old when God promised him that He would make Abram (before the name change) a great nation: "He [God] took him [Abram] outside and said, 'Look up at the sky and count the stars—if indeed you can count them. Then he said to him, 'So shall your offspring be'" (Genesis 15:5, NIV). But eleven years into waiting on the promise, they started to wonder: *What in the world is going on? How long do we have to wait?* Abraham is eighty-six years old now, and Sarah's not a spring chicken either. Out of frustration, Sarah suggested that Abraham father a child with her servant, Hagar (Genesis 16:1–4).

Anyone could understand them getting tired of waiting. After eleven years and no sign of anything happening, most people would cry, "How long, Lord, how long?" In this case, another fourteen years. Genesis 21 describes it: "Abraham was a hundred years old when his son Isaac was born to him. Sarah said, 'God has brought me laughter, and everyone who hears about this will laugh with me'" (vv. 5–6, NIV). In their season of waiting, there was doubt, fear, and even manipulation of the promise. It brought sad results too: the nations at war today with Israel are the offspring of Ishmael, the son of Abraham and Hagar. This emphasizes the truth that we aren't supposed to understand God's timing. He simply asks us to trust it.

We aren't supposed to understand God's timing. He simply asks us to trust it.

When I look back over my life and ministry, every time I've tried to manipulate God's calendar or rush His timing, it almost always creates larger problems. God doesn't need our help; He simply wants our trust. Remember that God hears and answers every prayer, not on our timetable but His, and not always with the answer we want to hear. But the good news is, His time is always the right time.

Peter put it best:

> *But do not forget this one thing, dear friends: With the Lord, a day is like a thousand years, and a thousand years are like a day. The Lord is not slow in keeping his promise, as some understand slowness. Instead, he is patient with you, not wanting anyone to perish, but everyone to come to repentance.* —2 Peter 3:8–9 (NIV)

If you remember nothing else about this chapter, remember this: God is an on-time promise keeper.

QUESTIONS FOR DISCUSSION

1) Have you ever received help from a faith community after the death of a loved one or a personal crisis? How did that make you feel?

2) Have you offered help to someone in need of moral support? How did that make you feel?

3) Have you ever had an experience like Dottie Peoples and been concerned about running late? How did God come through for you?

4) Are you still waiting for God to resolve a situation and wondering why He's so late? What can you do about that?

Chapter 6

GOING FOR A WALK

> *"But the boat was now in the middle of the sea, tossed by the waves, for the wind was contrary. Now in the fourth watch of the night Jesus went to them, walking on the sea."*
>
> —Matthew 14:24–25

The days I spent in the hospital following my accident reinforced a truth that I had preached many times: we never walk alone. Jesus always walks beside us through our storms. His presence was a lighthouse in my dark days, like a vivid, strong, shining beacon of hope and healing. Regardless of the severity of my circumstances, His presence was a constant, unchanging harbor of peace.

Keeping our eyes on this harbor is essential when facing difficulties. As I said in the introduction, vision keeps us moving forward. I no longer preach this because of what I gleaned from Bible college lessons and Scripture study, as valuable as those elements are to "rightly dividing the word of truth" (2 Timothy 2:15). I preach it because I lived it. I moved from fear and doubt to faith and strong belief.

How else can I explain not suffering today from any back pain, never needing any medication or muscle relaxers, nor struggling with nightmares because of my trip through such a traumatic experience? How else can I explain being able to run and ride my bike again when the doctors at the trauma center said they were going to keep a close eye on me because "95 percent of the time, that kind of injury requires surgery"? `Well, a 5 percent chance with God is better than 95 percent with the world.

> *A 5 percent chance with God is better than 95 percent with the world.*

Now, I don't guarantee that God will heal every person who suffers from an accident, a cancer diagnosis, or heart disease. For one, He is not just an on-time God. He is also a one-on-one God, dealing with us individually and bringing us what we need when we need it. Just as Isaiah said, His ways and thoughts are higher than ours. So, I can't explain every intricate detail of how He works. Nor why He does what He does. Yet because He brought me through this ordeal victoriously, I know He still walks on water. He is the same God who came to the disciples in the moment of their greatest fear.

COMING TO US

The disciples couldn't go to where Jesus was on the mountainside; He walked to them on the Sea of Galilee. When we can't go to

Him, He comes to us. When He comes to us *in our* storm, He comes to us *victorious over* it.

To appreciate what happened in the pre-dawn hours of that historic night, consider the full picture. The disciples were in the middle of the sea, with wind and waves beating against the boat. Not a modern cruise liner that is three football fields long and can carry hundreds of passengers. Try a small craft about 27 feet long, 7.5 feet wide, and 4.3 feet deep, with enough room for fifteen passengers.

I say "about" because nobody knows the exact dimensions of the boat the disciples were in that night. But in 1986, two fishermen from a kibbutz along the western shore of the Sea of Galilee discovered the hull of a fishing boat old enough to have been on the water in the first century. It was mired in the muddy lakebed during a time of severe drought, with radiocarbon dating verifying it originated as a fishing vessel between 120 BC and 40 AD—which spans the time Jesus spent on the Sea of Galilee. Says one account:

> *Excavating it safely presented a huge challenge to excavators. Conservation of its waterlogged timbers took eleven years. In 2000, the vessel—officially known as "The Ancient Galilee Boat"—went on permanent display in the Yigal Allon Museum at Kibbutz Ginosar, near where it was discovered.*[11]

No matter the boat's size, we know from Scripture that the disciples were sorely afraid of drowning in the raging waters. The Gospel of Mark contains another account of crossing the

---
11 "Jesus Boat," *See the Holy Land*, accessed October 16, 2023, https://www.seetheholyland.net/jesus-boat/.

Sea of Galilee, where the disciples allowed their fear to trump their faith. Chapter 4 describes Jesus and His disciples leaving a crowd behind to cross the lake. As they sailed alongside some other boats, Jesus fell asleep. Verse 37 describes a furious squall coming up, which sent waves crashing over the boat and nearly swamping it. And there lay Jesus, sleeping like a baby.

Mark continues:

> *The disciples woke him and said to him, "Teacher, don't you care if we drown?" He got up, rebuked the wind, and said to the waves, "Quiet! Be still!" Then, the wind died down, and it was completely calm. He said to his disciples, "Why are you so afraid? Do you still have no faith?" They were terrified and asked each other, "Who is this? Even the wind and the waves obey him!"* —vv. 38–41 (NIV, emphasis added)

To that, I would add, "Wow!" We should all try to place ourselves in the midst of this raging storm. It's no wonder the disciples were frantic. We'd be right beside them, yelling, "Hey, don't You see what's going on out here? We're gonna die!" It is so easy to feel like God is sleeping during the storms in our lives or to think He is indifferent to our circumstances. The disciples couldn't take it anymore, so they woke Him up to ask, "Teacher, don't you care if we drown?" When we take our eyes off what God is doing and put them on our circumstances, the storm will always deceive us and make us believe we are drowning. But Jesus will never allow us to drown.

> *When we take our eyes off what God is doing and put them on our circumstances, the storm will always deceive us and make us believe we are drowning.*

FORGETTING FAITHFULNESS

Fear causes us to forget God's faithfulness in our lives. Satan will always try to make us forget that God performs miracles and that He has promised us a life of abundance. He will come and try to steal away every victory we have ever had. That is natural because lying springs from his nature. Jesus told the Pharisees: "When he [the devil] speaks a lie, he speaks from his own resources, for he is a liar and the father of it" (John 8:44). Later, He added, "The thief comes to only steal and kill and destroy; I have come that they may have life and have it to the full" (John 10:10, NIV).

Jesus brings abundant life, which is seen in the Mark 4 passage. He awakens, gets up, rebukes the wind, and tells the waves to be still. He can do this because Jesus has authority over creation. When we're in a storm, we must remember that God can still the waves and calm the winds in the twinkling of an eye. He has already won the victory. We simply need to trust Him.

However, during the action described in Matthew 14 (and Mark 6), Jesus wasn't in the boat with them. Again, their hearts began to doubt. They were exhausted and afraid as they searched for a break in the clouds. Finally, they screamed for help, but they heard nothing. They started playing the same kind of "if only" games that we can today: *If only* Jesus were in the boat with them. *If only* they hadn't gone out so late. *If only* Jesus had told them to stay on the shore. But He was not in the boat and insisted they go before Him to the other side. Far from shore, they had been fighting the storm for hours and were exhausted by the struggle. Likewise, storms can dominate our lives, overtaking us and making us think they will never end.

But then . . . just when all hope was lost, Jesus came to them, walking on the water. He came victorious to calm their fear of drowning. Water could not drown them, it could not destroy them, and it could not defeat them because it was under the feet of Jesus!

Today, He comes to us as captain of our storm, victorious and triumphant.

To the sick, He comes as healer: "By his wounds you have been healed" (1 Peter 2:24, NIV).

To the needy, He comes as provider: "But my God shall supply all your need according to his riches in glory by Christ Jesus" (Philippians 4:19, KJV).

To the bound, He comes as the deliverer: "Stand fast therefore in the liberty by which Christ has made us free, and do not be entangled again with a yoke of bondage" (Galatians 5:1).

To the grieving, He comes as the comforter:

> *Blessed be the God and Father of our Lord Jesus Christ, the Father of mercies and God of all comfort, who comforts us in all our tribulation, that we may be able to comfort those who are in any trouble, with the comfort with which we ourselves are comforted by God.* —2 Corinthians 1:3–4

To the lost, He comes as redeemer: "For the Son of Man has come to seek and to save that which was lost" (Luke 19:10).

The best news for everyone is He has already won the victory. As Paul wrote to the church at Corinth: "But thanks be to God! He gives us the victory through our Lord Jesus Christ" (1 Corinthians 15:57, NIV). This is the kind of Savior who comes to us in our storms and is our confidence in times of trouble. He will never abandon us. To quote Paul's letter to the Corinthians again:

> *We are troubled on every side, yet not distressed; we are perplexed, but not in despair; persecuted, but not forsaken; cast down, but not destroyed; always bearing about in the body the dying of the Lord Jesus, that the life also of Jesus might be made manifest in our body. —2 Corinthians 4:8–10 (KJV)*

A CONSTANT PRESENCE

Because of tightened hospital visitation during the pandemic, my family could only be by my bedside for a limited number of hours: 10:00 a.m. to 6:00 p.m. Only a maximum of two persons per day were allowed in, and everyone who came in had to wear a wristband. But God is not limited by a hospital's visiting procedures. He is an ever-present help in time of need. He is with us every step of the journey. This is why the writer of Hebrews said, "Be happy with what you have because God has said, 'I will never abandon you or leave you'" (Hebrews 13:5, GW). Whatever the storm, we do not face it alone. We should not place our security in our money, talent, resources, intelligence, or family name. We are secure because He walks with us through our storm.

During this season, the Lord taught me how to rest in Him. This was difficult for me because my personality is "to do." I often struggle with resting and waiting on God. As you likely recognize, I want immediate action, hence my story in chapter 5 about getting impatient at the McDonald's drive-through window. I want a plan and a path. But I learned a lesson during my extended hospital stay—sometimes we must just trust in the Lord. We all face circumstances over which we have no control and seasons when our only option is to trust our ever-present help in time of need.

We all face circumstances over which we have no control and seasons when our only option is to trust our ever-present help in time of need.

I learned three key lessons in the early days of my accident. I had preached these truths throughout my ministry and taught these lessons in Bible classes and Sunday school on many occasions. But I was now living them out.

1) Prayer accomplishes more than worry.

Whenever an anxious thought filled my mind, I would pray, worship, and give thanks. I would stand on God's promises: "Be anxious for nothing, but in everything by prayer and supplication, with thanksgiving, let your requests be made known to God; and the peace of God, which surpasses all understanding, will guard your hearts and minds through Christ Jesus" (Philippians 4:6–7).

2) Jesus hasn't changed.

He is the same yesterday, today, and forever. That constant presence offers peace and reassurance in a world where anything can be taken away in a flash of time. Immediately after my accident, many friends encouraged us that everything was going to be alright. But I also knew that, although that is what we were praying for, there was the possibility that I wouldn't be healed. I might be disabled or permanently need to wear a back brace, moving around when I could in only slow and agonizing steps. Or become bedridden, forced into a dependent state for the rest of my life. But even if things didn't work out like we prayed, Jesus Christ stays the same. That powerful, comforting truth sustained me through those times when the devil attacked with all the lies and doubts he could hurl at me.

3) He is my firm foundation.

When the uncertainties of life overwhelm us, our dependence on God must increase. We should say as David did, "From the ends of the earth, I cry out to you for help when my heart is overwhelmed. Lead me to the towering rock of safety, for you are my safe refuge, a fortress where my enemies cannot reach me" (Psalm 61:2–3, NLT). We stand on the unshakeable, unchanging, and unmovable rock that is Jesus Christ. When we rest in Jesus, we are safe. This is why David asked God to lead him to the towering rock of safety, out of reach of the evils that can cause us to sink.

RUN TO THE ROCK

This is a lesson I learned in a new and remarkable way during the aftermath of my accident—when the strong winds blow, we must run to the Rock. I began running to the Rock to avoid being consumed by uncertainty. I discovered that when we do this and dark clouds fill the skies, we will not constantly worry. We will find shelter in His truth and depend upon His strong arm. While we may not know how things will turn out, we keep our eyes on the One who does. Trust in Jesus because He will neither leave nor forsake us. He will always be the solid Rock on which we can stand and withstand the fierce winds, hail, rain, and debris stirred up by the storm.

Knowing that Jesus Christ, our Lord and Savior, neither leaves nor abandons us is a true assurance. This is such a tremendous promise from God (which Moses first wrote about in Deuteronomy 31) that we cannot underestimate its power: "He will be with you, He will not leave you nor forsake you; do not fear nor be dismayed" (v. 8).

Those words are similar to what the Lord told Joshua after he took Moses's place as the leader of Israel: "Have I not commanded you? Be strong and of good courage; do not be afraid, nor be dismayed, for the LORD your God is with you wherever you go" (Joshua 1:9). It is why the prophet Isaiah wrote, "Fear not, for I am with you; be not dismayed, for I am your God. I will strengthen you, yes, I will help you, I will uphold you with My righteous right hand" (Isaiah 41:10). And why David could write, "Cast your burden on the LORD, and He shall sustain you; He shall never permit the righteous to be moved" (Psalm 55:22), and "In God (I will praise His word), in God I have put my trust; I will not fear. What can flesh do to me?" (Psalm 56:4).

We will all find ourselves in helpless, difficult, or challenging situations. Too often, we try to fix or work out these situations by our reasoning, logic, or efforts. We also often find that despite all our attempts to fix the problem, there seems to be no hope of help. These difficult times often drive us to take drastic measures. When going through these hard seasons, it is easy to allow the voice of our doubt to drown out everything else: *We just need to get out of this storm!* However, at such times, we must remember that because Jesus is always with us, we are never alone.

ABIDING LOVE

From personal experience, I know it isn't always easy to stand when the battles of life are raging around us, but we can rest assured in the promise that God loves and will not forsake us. Psalm 37:28 says, "For the LORD loves justice; he will not forsake his saints. They are preserved forever, but the children of the wicked shall be cut off" (ESV). He is always with us to save us from the attacks of the enemy.

First Peter 5:8 tells us that the enemy roars at us like a lion as he seeks victims to devour, but the devil cannot harm us. God has given us strength and empowered us to overcome the enemy. He assures us in His Word: "Be strong and of good courage, do not fear nor be afraid of them; for the LORD your God, He is the One who goes with you. He will not leave you nor forsake you" (Deuteronomy 31:6). God has not abandoned us.

David described His continual presence this way:

If I go up to the heavens, you are there; if I make my bed in the depths, you are there. If I rise on the wings of the dawn, if I settle on the far side of the sea, even there your hand will guide me, your right hand will hold me fast. —Psalm 139:8–10 (NIV)

Jesus didn't tell the disciples to come to Him. He knew they couldn't get to Him. So, He went to them. Jesus didn't stand on the shore and shout instructions on how to row a boat in a storm. The disciples didn't need advice; they needed a miracle! They needed Jesus to show up and intervene in the storm. That's what Jesus did: He showed up!

This is a picture of the gospel: God doesn't stand on the shoreline telling us what to do. Instead, He comes out and meets us in our storm—in our sin, pain, fear, depression, and discouragement; He comes to us. Jesus said, "I will not abandon you or leave you as orphans in the storm—I will come to you" (John 14:18, TLB). He will never leave us.

This is a picture of the gospel: God doesn't stand on the shoreline telling us what to do. Instead, He comes out and meets us in our storm—in our sin, pain, fear, depression, and discouragement; He comes to us.

The psalmist assures us of God's love and care with these words: "Out of my distress I called on the LORD; the LORD answered me and set me free. The LORD is on my side; I will not fear. What can man do to me?" (Psalm 118:5–6, ESV). I know exactly what he meant. I called out to God, "in my distress," and "the Lord answered me and set me free." Lori and I were able to make it through our storm because the Lord was at our side. As the psalmist declared, He was "on my side" all the time, even if I didn't see Him. Likewise, He will be there for us in our greatest time of need.

QUESTIONS FOR DISCUSSION

1) How do you "rightly divide the word of truth" (2 Timothy 2:15)?

2) Have you ever battled fear or nervousness about a situation at work? How did God help you through that time?

3) Have you ever said, "If only... this hadn't happened, then this other thing... wouldn't have happened"? What is the end result of this kind of fretting?

4) How does God supply your needs? Have you ever thanked Him? Why?

Chapter 7

LIGHT IN THE DARKNESS

> *"And when the disciples saw Him walking on the sea,* they were troubled, *saying,* 'It is a ghost!' *And they* cried out for fear. *But immediately* Jesus spoke *to them, saying,* 'Be of good cheer! *It is* I; do not be afraid.'"
>
> —Matthew 14:26–27 (emphasis added)

When I walked in the front door the morning the unknown motorist smashed into my bicycle, feelings of terror gripped Lori. She spent much of that day trying to wrap her head around what had happened. As she drove toward the hospital, I gestured and said, "This is the way the guy was bringing me." At this point, she didn't know all the details of what had just happened, so she thought, *He's talking out of his head.* Then she asked, "What guy? What are you talking about?"

It hadn't occurred to her that there was no way I could have ridden my mangled bicycle home from the accident scene three miles away. That's when I related the story of how I had come to consciousness in the front seat of this guy's pickup truck. After I described exactly what had happened and how I directed the mystery man who drove me to our house, Lori realized I had my wits about me. She was able to relax a little then, although still unnerved by this unexpected interruption to our lives.

While I eventually recovered from the accident with body and spirit intact, in the days immediately following it, I confess to sometimes feeling a bit bewildered, alone, and afraid. Typically, when we head across town to visit a sick friend, we may not think much about the emotions surging through their mind right then. After all, we're in a familiar place where we know lots of folks, the layout of the streets, and many of the buildings on the blocks surrounding the hospital.

I didn't feel so comfortable being two hours away from home. Lori, our children, and a few friends were the only faces I recognized. Since I made the trip while lying flat on my back in an ambulance, I had little sense of exactly where I was and how I had gotten there.

One night, as I lay there, alone with my thoughts and battling fear, I asked God, "Where are you?" The answer quickly came back in the form of a voice so small I barely heard it, yet so loud it's as if it came blasting through a megaphone: *I never left. Rejoice; don't be afraid. You're not alone; I AM with you in the storm.*

I encouraged myself in the multiple promises from His Word (which I reviewed in chapter 6) that He will never leave us or forsake us. While I may have doubted His presence momentarily, He was still there. While I sometimes struggled to hear His voice, He still spoke. While I am a flawed human being, He understands my weaknesses. It's so reassuring to recall what Paul told Timothy, "If we are faithless, He remains faithful; He cannot deny Himself" (2 Timothy 2:13). And what David wrote in the

Psalms: "You keep track of all my sorrows. You have collected all my tears in your bottle. You have recorded each one in your book" (Psalm 56:8, NLT).

He sees, He knows, and He understands what we are going through. He is our peace during the storm.

He sees, He knows, and He understands what we are going through. He is our peace during the storm: "I have told you these things, so that in me you may have peace. In this world you will have trouble. But take heart! I have overcome the world" (John 16:33, NIV).

STRUGGLING TO SEE

The most challenging time to see Jesus is in the midst of a storm. But whether we see Him, recognize His voice, or even acknowledge His presence, Jesus is still with us. I like how scholar Albert Lee put it in a devotional for *Our Daily Bread*:

> *No one is exempt from the storms of life. But just as the disciples who initially feared the storm later came to revere Christ more, the storms we face can bring us to a deeper knowledge of God. . . . Through our trials, we can learn that no storm is big enough to prevent God from accomplishing His will. While we may not understand why God allows trials to enter our lives, we*

thank Him that we can come to know who He is through them. We live to serve Him because He has preserved our lives.[12]

While those are encouraging words, we can be so deep in the storm and overtaken by the darkness of the clouds that we think no one knows, no one cares, and no one understands. If you have ever felt this way, that puts you in good company—right next to the disciples as they struggled to stay alive on the Sea of Galilee.

Fortunately, Jesus understands our doubts and fears. He didn't get offended when He came to the disciples in the middle of the storm, and they didn't recognize His presence. Since they were terrified, one can wonder, *Would they recognize His voice?* He spoke to them: "Be joyful, it is I; don't be afraid." But they couldn't see Him through the storm. They couldn't hear over their fear. The disciples thought that circumstances couldn't get any worse. Fear often causes us to imagine, perceive, and even believe God has abandoned us in our hour of trouble.

Fear had so clouded their minds that even though they saw Jesus walking on the water, they thought He was an apparition. Maybe the angel of death had come with his icy grip, and they would die on the water. The storm was so dark and imposing they couldn't see the Giver of Life walking on the sea. The disciples allowed doubt to blind their eyes to the One who came with abundant life.

But as the familiar promotional campaign says, "He gets us." He understands our insecurities and unbelief. Despite the disciples' lack of faith, He ministered to them. Jesus encouraged them

---

[12] Albert Lee, "The Storms of Life," *Our Daily Bread*, accessed October 19, 2023, https://ourdailybread.org/article/the-storms-of-life/.

to rejoice and not be afraid. He spoke peace in the midst of their storm. When you engage in such behavior and insist everything will be fine when it looks like the world is crashing down around you, more than one friend or coworker will mutter under their breath, "Sounds like they're crazy."

However, as I pointed out previously, Hebrews 11:1 says faith is the substance of things we hope for and the evidence of things we can't yet see. So, to believe in a Spirit we can't taste, touch, or snap a selfie with does sometimes appear like craziness. To have joy when there appears to be little to be joyful about? That may seem unbelievable until you consider the literal translation of what Jesus said: "Be joyful, I AM; don't be afraid."

I AM is God's name. When God appeared to Moses in the burning bush and told him to go to Egypt to lead the Israelites out of slavery, Moses said,

> *Indeed, when I come to the children of Israel and say to them, "The God of your fathers has sent me to you, and they say to me, 'What is His name?' what shall I say to them?" And God said to Moses, "I AM WHO I AM." And He said, "Thus you shall say to the children of Israel, 'I AM has sent me to you.'" —Exodus 3:13–14*

The phrase "I am" in Hebrew was ubiquitous in the language and was used in everyday conversation: "I am watching the children," "I am cleaning the house," or "I am your father." But, when used by God as a stand-alone description, *I AM* is a declaration of self-sufficiency and self-existence. God's existence is not dependent upon anyone else. Circumstances do not determine

His plans. God promises that He will be eternally constant and consistent. He is entirely self-sufficient in Himself to do what He wills to do.

ALPHA AND OMEGA

When God referred to Himself as I AM WHO I AM, He was declaring that He is the sovereign Creator, the beginning and the end: "'I am the Alpha and the Omega,' says the Lord God, 'who is, and who was, and who is to come, the Almighty'" (Revelation 1:8, NIV).

I AM is a declaration of sovereignty and power. When we wonder if God is coming, He answers with His name: "I AM!" When we wonder if He is able, He declares, "I AM." When we see overwhelming darkness, feel nothing but fear, and doubt if God is even aware of our circumstances, the answer is "I AM!" The secret to joy in the storm is "I AM." Jesus said, "Be joyful." Our joy is not based on our circumstances but in the great "I AM."

Our greatest need in every storm is His presence. We want this storm to pass. We want the winds to still. But we need to know that the great I AM is always with us, assuring us:

> *"Don't be afraid, I've redeemed you. I've called your name. You're mine. When you're in over your head, I'll be there with you.* When you're in rough waters, you will not go down.... *I am GOD, your personal God, the Holy of Israel, your Savior. ... So don't be afraid: I'm with you." —Isaiah 43:2–5 (MSG)*

Naturally, we all would rather be spared the storm. But if the storm comes, our prayer is usually, "Let it be light and, God, be quick to deliver us." But when that doesn't happen and we're in the middle of a raging storm, Jesus says, "I AM with you, and I will see you through." Whether we see Him or not, He is working. Whether we feel Him, He's working. This reality is one reason I enjoy the song "Way Maker," which proclaims repeatedly in melodious harmonies that He never stops working.[13]

Sometimes, I wonder if Christ's followers truly appreciate the riches that each of us has in His death, burial, resurrection, and the eternal life that follows for all who embrace His sacrifice. While Hebrews 4:14–16 has always been a favorite passage, I especially like how *The Message* paraphrases it:

> *Now that we know what we have—Jesus, this great High Priest with ready access to God—let's not let it slip through our fingers. We don't have a priest who is out of touch with our reality. He's been through weakness and testing, experienced it all—all but the sin. So, let's walk right up to him and get what He is so ready to give. Take the mercy, accept the help.*

WHY HE UNDERSTANDS

Jesus understands our struggles, our pain, and our weaknesses and ministers to us where we are for multiple reasons:

He endured temptation: "He was in the desert forty days, being tempted by Satan" (Mark 1:13, NIV). Jesus understands the pressures of temptation since He was tempted in every way, just like we are, but without sinning. Jesus has been there and can relate to us based on His humanity. Philippians tells us that

---

[13] Leeland, vocalist, "Way Maker" by Osinachi Kalu Okoro, August 16, 2019, track 3 on *Better Word*, Integrity Music.

he emptied Himself of everything and entered into mankind in human form: "Who, being in the form of God, did not consider it robbery to be equal with God, but made Himself of no reputation, taking the form of a bondservant, and coming in the likeness of men" (Philippians 2:6–7). In other words, He surrendered all His divine privileges and became a man. Jesus did this for us so we could have abundant life.

Jesus understands our struggles, our pain, and our weaknesses and ministers to us where we are.

Jesus was raised in poverty: "And Jesus said to him, 'Foxes have holes and birds of the air have nests, but the Son of Man has nowhere to lay His head'" (Matthew 8:20). He knew the struggles of life and experienced the pain of lack. He knew the pain of poverty. Jesus started with nothing after being born in the humblest of circumstances. Born to teenage parents in a manger surrounded by animals. The King of Kings and Lord of Lords was not born in a palace, and He did not live a life of luxury.

Jesus was ridiculed: "Again and again they struck him ... and spit on him. Falling on their knees, they paid [mocking] homage to him" (Mark 15:19, NIV). Jesus had a human body, exactly like ours, and so was capable of feeling pain. He knew the shame of being mocked by others. Because He was mocked and ridiculed, He understands our suffering.

Jesus experienced loneliness: "My God, my God, why have You forsaken Me?" (Matthew 27:46). Jesus was a sinless, perfect person living in a sinful world. No one on earth could identify with Him. His parents, siblings, relatives, and friends were all conceived in sin. His status as a divine and sinless human left Him alone. But Jesus's loneliness reached its peak on the cross when He became sin for us and was "forsaken" by his Father. He was estranged from God when He became sin for us. Jesus knew rejection and loneliness. Jesus doesn't just understand our loneliness; He sacrificed so that we would never walk alone. He promised that "I will never leave you nor forsake you" (Hebrews 13:5).

Jesus faced frustration: He understands our frustrations and even our anger. He is not so far removed from our life experiences that He cannot connect with us where we live. We can see this in His reaction to the merchants turning what was a place dedicated to worshiping His Father into a marketplace for buying and selling goods:

> *He drove them all out of the temple, with the sheep and the oxen, and poured out the changers' money and overturned the tables. And He said to those who sold doves, "Take these things away! Do not make My Father's house a house of merchandise!"* —John 2:15–16

Jesus knew weariness: "Jesus, tired as he was from the journey, sat down by the well" (John 4:6 NIV). The word "tired" (or "wearied") in this verse means to labor until worn out or depleted. He was not just a little tired; He was exhausted. We all have days that leave us exhausted. You know the feeling of those days when our physical and emotional strength are gone, and we are just weary. When we are so tired, we collapse into the nearest chair, drained from the day's challenges and feeling worn out; we wonder how we can get up and do it again tomorrow. Fortunately, we serve a Savior who understands our weariness.

Jesus dealt with disappointment: "O Jerusalem, Jerusalem ... How often I wanted to gather your children together, as a hen gathers her brood . . . but you were not willing!" (Luke 13:34). We have all been disappointed by people—people who left when the heat got turned up, betrayed a confidence, or who hurt us when they could have helped us. Jesus experienced the pain of such disappointment.

Jesus endured rejection: "From this time many of his disciples turned back and no longer followed him" (John 6:66, NIV). Rejection has visited all of us, but never like it did the Messiah. Centuries before His birth, the prophet Isaiah wrote of Jesus: "He is despised and rejected by men, a Man of sorrows and acquainted with grief. And we hid, as it were, our faces from Him; He was despised, and we did not esteem Him" (Isaiah 53:3).

Jesus felt sorrow: He knew anguish; at the tomb of Lazarus, He wept. In the garden of Gethsemane, He told His disciples, "My soul is overwhelmed with sorrow to the point of death" (Matthew 26:38, NIV). He understands our sorrow and pain. We are not alone. No matter what we go through, we have a God who is "intimately acquainted" with all our ways (Psalm 139:3, NASB 1995). He doesn't stand back from our pain. Instead, He wants to shine light into the darkest part of our lives.

ONE WHO UNDERSTANDS

You may think no one else understands—not your husband or wife, children, siblings, coworkers, or other church members. But He understands. He has heard every late-night prayer and seen every tear that has rolled down your cheek. He understands what we're going through and ministers to us right where we are. To revisit Isaiah's prophecy in a fuller dimension:

> *He was despised and rejected by mankind,*
> *a man of suffering and familiar with pain.*
> *Like one from whom people hide their faces*
> *he was despised, and we held him in low esteem.*
> *Surely he took up our pain*
> *and bore our suffering,*
> *yet we considered him punished by God,*
> *stricken by him, and afflicted.*
> *But he was pierced for our transgressions,*
> *he was crushed for our iniquities;*
> *the punishment that brought us peace was on him,*
> *and by his wounds we are healed.* —Isaiah 53:3–5 (NIV)

Regardless of the valley's depth or the storm's intensity, He understands our struggles, fears, and pain.

Regardless of the valley's depth or the storm's intensity, He understands our struggles, fears, and pain. He bore our pains and sorrows so that we could know unspeakable joy in the storm. We have a Savior who is real and present in His children's lives, so we do not have to fear.

QUESTIONS FOR DISCUSSION

1) Have you felt alone and/or afraid in a strange place? What helped you overcome those feelings?

2) Have you ever meditated on how Christ endured the devil's temptations in Matthew 4:1–11? What can we learn from His example?

3) Jesus was betrayed by Judas, one of the twelve disciples. Has a close friend ever betrayed you? Were you able to forgive them? Explain.

4) Have you ever felt rejected like Jesus was in John 6:66? How can prayer help you get over the anguish?

Chapter 8
WHAT'S IT LIKE TO SINK?

> *"And Peter answered Him and said, 'Lord, if it is You, command me to come to You on the water.' So He said, 'Come.' And when Peter had come down out of the boat, he walked on the water to go to Jesus. But when he saw that the wind was boisterous, he was afraid; and beginning to sink he cried out, saying, 'Lord, save me!' And immediately Jesus stretched out His hand and caught him, and said to him, 'O you of little faith, why did you doubt?'"*
>
> —Matthew 14:28–31

In chapter 6, I mentioned being able to run and ride my bike again after the doctors at the trauma center said they were going to keep a close eye on me because 95 percent of the time that kind of injury requires surgery. That statement may have sounded more confident than I really felt when I first heard those words. To give a full accounting of one doctor's statement: "Ninety-five percent of the patients I see with your injuries require surgery. There is a possibility of being paralyzed or at least the loss of mobility and the probability of a lifetime of pain."

As I lay there in my hospital bed and meditated on his gloomy prognosis, I asked, "God, why?" It was a question I asked multiple times in the first few days following my accident. But I learned a life-changing lesson in that unknown season: no matter what it looks like, no matter what bills are due, no matter what sickness, death, or other circumstances we are facing, we should always view them in the light of His love. We should never view His love in the light of our circumstances!

> *We should never view His love in the light of our circumstances!*

His love is greater, deeper, wider, higher than my storm. My "Why?" would soon turn to "Who." The *who* is far greater than the *why*. The who is a God who loves me more than I can grasp or comprehend. I can confidently say that because I rely on the words of Scripture, not my brilliance or my experience. As John wrote, "This is real love—not that we loved God, but that he loved us and sent his Son as a sacrifice to take away our sins" (1 John 4:10, NLT). Paul wrote to the church at Rome: "But God demonstrates His own love toward us, in that while we were still sinners, Christ died for us" (Romans 5:8).

Long before Lori and I lifted our hands in worship, before we ever responded to the call to ministry, even before we knew Him, He knew us and loved us! Before we served, gave, or attended a church, He loved us! His love is so vast that it covers all of creation. Saints and sinners are equal recipients of God's great love. The only question we must answer is whether we will accept that love.

DETERMINING OUR FAITH

We can be assured of Christ's love by examining what happened with the disciples in general and Peter in particular. As their boat tossed on the waves, the disciples overflowed with doubt. The situation looked hopeless. Most of the disciples seemed helpless amid their waves of fear and shallow faith.

But Peter didn't allow the storm to determine his faith—he looked past it and saw Jesus. Despite his apprehension, Peter gathered the faith to ask, "Lord, if it is (really) You, command me to come to You on the water." Without hesitating, Jesus said, "Come"; He will always say, "Come." Apply that to whatever sickness, troubled child, overbearing boss, or financial worry you are facing right now, and remember that He is the Master of the sea, Creator of the wind, and Ruler of the universe. He is our Lord, Jesus Christ. It may seem like the boat is being tossed from stem to stern and is nowhere near a safe place, but He says, "Come." No matter how impossible it may seem, He says, "Come." The situation may not make sense, but He says, "Come."

> *He will always say, "Come." Apply that to whatever sickness, troubled child, overbearing boss, or financial worry you are facing right now.*

It was Jesus who made His disciples get in the boat and go before Him to the other side of the Sea of Galilee. But now the focus shifted from getting in the boat to getting out of the boat. Peter had to get out of the boat. The miracle was waiting for him on the water. Peter got out of the boat despite the towering winds and giant waves. Likewise, we can't wait for the seas to calm and the storm to pass to test the waters. Sometimes, you just have to get out of the boat. Fear will tell us that we're going to sink with the ship. But faith declares even if the ship sinks, our hope is not in a manmade boat but in the power of God.

> *Fear will tell us that we're going to sink with the ship. But faith declares even if the ship sinks, our hope is not in a manmade boat but in the power of God.*

This is why Jesus called Peter to come to Him on the water. Peter obeyed. We must realize that we can never walk on water if we never get out of the boat. This miracle was spectacular and has been retold in books, movies, and paintings an untold number of times. It was portrayed recently in the final episode of *The Chosen*, the crowd-funded TV series about Jesus that has circulated worldwide. The first three seasons were picked up for nationwide broadcasts on the CW network in the latter half of 2023.[14]

Writing about how much he loved this episode (which was shown in theaters and not just via streaming), one high school journalist wrote,

> *The best part of episode eight came at the end. (The) crowd is fed with the multiplied loaves and fishes, and the disciples and Jesus are left to travel back to Capernaum. The disciples traveled back on the water, getting caught in a rough storm. At first, while watching, I thought it was just a side plot, but as lightning strikes, John . . . sees a figure coming towards the boat on the water. Soon, they realize it is not a ghost, but Jesus walking on the water towards them.*
>
> *I was absolutely blown away by this portrayal of such an iconic moment, and I was on the edge of my seat the entire time. I had no clue it was going to be in the finale episode, even after watching multiple trailers, but frankly, the surprise made the scene even more impactful. From Jesus commanding Simon to walk on water, and Simon finally letting his grief get the best of him and falling in, to Jesus saving Simon and commanding the storm to stop, the classic story was told in such a powerful way it was impossible not to cry.*[15]

---

14 *The Chosen*, Dallas Jenkins, December 4, 2017, Angel Studios.
15 Sammie Jo Clark, "Season three finale of 'The Chosen' creates waves in the box office," *The Brantley Banner*, 28 Feb. 2023, https://brantleybanner.com/12573/arts-and-entertainment/season-three-finale-of-the-chosen-creates-waves-in-the-box-office/.

JESUS, THE OVERCOMER

No matter how exhilarating the cinema or astonishing the event it portrayed, the lesson here is much bigger than the miracle: because Jesus has overcome, we can also overcome. Peter walked victoriously on the water because Jesus had already won the victory. This is why He told His disciples, "I have told you all this so that you may have peace in me. Here on earth, you will have many trials and sorrows. But take heart, because I have overcome the world" (John 16:33, NLT). Those words were echoed by the apostle John in his first letter: "You, dear children, are from God and have overcome them, because the one who is in you is greater than the one who is in the world" (1 John 4:4, NIV).

However, circumstances can blind us to our victory in Jesus, with dark clouds and strong winds distracting us. Peter started to sink when he took his eyes off Jesus and put them on the storm. Matthew 14:30 recounts: "When he saw that the wind was boisterous, he was afraid."

Circumstances can be scary. A negative diagnosis from the doctor, not enough money to pay the bills, a life-altering tragedy like a death in our family, a devastating loss, or other storms can cause us to take our gaze off Jesus. When we allow fear to rule, it diminishes our faith. But where faith rules, it drives fear away. Faith and fear don't mix. When we bring in faith, fear will disappear. When life is a storm, look for Jesus and keep your eyes on Him. Faith releases the supernatural. It was when Peter trusted God that he stepped out of the boat and walked on the water. Fear will cause us to sink. When Peter had faith, he walked on water. When he was afraid, he sank in the water. Fear will sink us; faith will raise us up.

Faith is simply taking the next step. Peter took one step to get out of the boat and onto the water. Peter was doing it! Walking on water when he focused on Jesus and sinking into trouble when he lost sight of the Master of the Sea. As Peter was sinking in the water, Jesus immediately reached out (there's that word, "immediately," again) and caught him. His love reaches to us in our lowest lows and highest highs.

> *Whether we are walking on the water or sinking in it, He is the Master of the storm. And through Him, we are more than victorious.*

A picture of God's great love is woven throughout this passage from Matthew 14. After catching him, Jesus says to Peter that he has "little faith." Jesus knew Peter was capable of even greater faith. In contrast, the disciples in the boat had no faith. He is bigger than our fears, and He will not let us sink. Whether we are walking on the water or sinking in it, He is the Master of the storm. And through Him, we are more than victorious:

> *Jesus said to him, "If you can believe, all things are possible to him who believes." Immediately the father of the child cried out and said with tears, "Lord, I believe; help my unbelief!" —Mark 9:23–24*

> *So, Jesus said to them, "Because of your unbelief; for assuredly, I say to you, if you have faith as a mustard seed, you will say to this mountain, 'Move from here to there,' and it will move; and nothing will be impossible for you."* —Matthew 17:20

> *So Jesus answered and said to them, "Assuredly, I say to you, if you have faith and do not doubt, you will not only do what was done to the fig tree, but also if you say to this mountain, 'Be removed and be cast into the sea,' it will be done. And whatever things you ask in prayer, believing, you will receive."* —Matthew 21:21–22

CHANGE OF FORTUNES

As I discovered coming through my accident and the rehabilitation that followed, it is much easier to talk about faith and overcoming once the storm has passed than while the winds are still howling. Lest we be too critical of the disciples, let us consider the day they had just experienced. It began with sunny, cloudless skies and thousands of people flocking to the Master's side just to hear Jesus. Then the Savior miraculously fed thousands with a young boy's lunch. And suddenly, the disciples are being tossed by winds and waves, fighting for their lives. Why would Jesus send them out on the water without going with them? Didn't He care about what was happening? When things get difficult, and we find ourselves in a dark place, often our first response is one of doubt or questioning of His love.

This is why we need to be meditating daily on God's Word and fellowshipping regularly with other saints and fellow church members. We need each other! We need constant reminders of God's love, as expressed in this passage from Paul's first letter to Timothy:

> *Do not neglect the spiritual gift you received through the prophecy spoken over you when the elders of the church laid their hands on you. Give your complete attention to these matters. Throw yourself into your tasks so that everyone will see your progress. Keep a close watch on how you live and on your teaching. Stay true to what is right for the sake of your own salvation and the salvation of those who hear you. —1 Timothy 4:14–16 (NLT)*

In writing to the church in Rome, Paul offered a similar message as he described the unchanging, enduring, unending, matchless love of God:

> *Who shall separate us from the love of Christ? Shall tribulation, or distress, or persecution, or famine, or nakedness, or peril, or sword? . . . Yet in all these things, we are more than conquerors through Him who loved us. For I am persuaded that neither death nor life, nor angels nor principalities nor powers, nor things present nor things to come, nor height nor depth, nor any other created thing, shall be able to separate us from the love of God which is in Christ Jesus our Lord. —Romans 8:35, 37–39*

There is nothing that can prevent God from loving us. His love overcomes the power of Satan and the grip of death. His love strengthens us when we are persecuted and sustains us when we are tried. Nothing in this life or the life hereafter can stop Him from loving us: "Give thanks to the Lord, for he is good; his love endures forever" (1 Chronicles 16:34, NIV); "Because your love is better than life, my lips will glorify you" (Psalm 63:3, NIV).

> *Life without God's love is unimaginable;*
> *it's better than life itself.*

His love is cause for rejoicing. Life without His love is unimaginable; it's better than life itself. Our worship rises from His love in our hearts. As the prophet Isaiah wrote:

> *"Though the mountains be shaken, and the hills be removed, yet my unfailing love for you will not be shaken nor my covenant of peace be removed," says the Lord, who has compassion on you. —Isaiah 54:10 (NIV)*

HIS VAST LOVE

Paul's words emphasize the clarion message: He loves us! More than we will ever comprehend or grasp. I discovered that during the time I lay in my hospital bed and in the weeks and months that followed when other storms arose. This is what the disciples discovered on the Sea of Galilee in ways that so moved them that—when followed by Jesus's death on the cross and His resurrection—most of them would die a martyr's death. They had experienced a perfect man worth living their lives for, no matter what the cost.

I love the words of the hymn found scribbled on the walls of a mentally ill patient at an insane asylum after his death:

Could we with ink the ocean fill and were the skies of parchment made; were every stalk on earth a quill, and every man a scribe by trade: to write the love of God above, would drain the ocean dry, nor could the scroll contain the whole though stretched from sky to sky.[16]

Two hundred years later, it would be the inspiration for the beautiful hymn "The Love of God," written by Frederick M. Lehman. An unknown historian would later write:

These words were found written on a cell wall in a prison some 200 years ago. It is not known why the prisoner was incarcerated; neither is it known if the words were original or if he had heard them somewhere and had decided to put them in a place where he could be reminded of the greatness of God's love—whatever the circumstances, he wrote them on the wall of his prison cell. In due time, he died and the men who had the job of repainting his cell were impressed by the words. Before their paint brushes had obliterated them, one of the men jotted them down and thus they were preserved.[17]

This is the love that Paul wanted everyone to experience; his prayer for the church at Ephesus is the same for us today:

That Christ may dwell in your hearts through faith; that you, being rooted and grounded in love, may be

---

16 Found in "Music of the Message: The Story of 'The Love of God,'" *Ministry Magazine*, September 1950, https://www.ministrymagazine.org/archive/1950/09/the-story-of-the-love-of-god.
17 Eve, "Frederick M. Lehman and 'The Love of God,'" *Westpark Baptist Church*, 2 Feb. 2020, https://westpark-baptist.com/frederick-m-lehman/.

> *able to comprehend with all the saints what is the width and length and depth and height—to know the love of Christ which passes knowledge; that you may be filled with all the fullness of God. —Ephesians 3:17–19*

There's another dimension to this picture. The love of Christ moves in all directions. Paul saw it as wide and long and high and deep. His love is expansive and unending. The apostle was teaching that the love of Christ:

Is wide. It is wide enough for the whole world, Jew and Gentile alike. No one is beyond the scope of His love.

Is long. It has been established from the foundation of the world.

Is high. Through His love, we are raised up to be seated with Christ in the heavenly places. The love of Christ is deep, meaning there is no sin too awful or trespass too severe to separate us from His love. Paul prayed for us to understand the love that Jesus has for us. Regardless of where life's journey takes us, we are completely overwhelmed by the relentless love of Jesus.

Is **unchanging.** First John 4:8 tells us, "God is love." He loves us! He always has and He always will. He loves us with an everlasting love. His love trumps our circumstances, overcomes our storms, and endures through the darkest night.

God's love trumps our circumstances, overcomes our storms, and endures through the darkest night.

I know this not just because He came to me during my darkest days in the hospital but in all the days that followed. That is something worth shouting about!

QUESTIONS FOR DISCUSSION

1) Has Jesus ever asked you to step into what seemed like an impossible situation? What happened?

2) What is a storm during the past year that caused you to take your eyes off Jesus? How did you weather the storm?

3) Have you ever thought about the width, length, depth, and height of God's love? What kind of images did that bring to mind?

4) What triumph in your life, your family's life, or a friend's life is worth shouting about?

Chapter 9

WHEN GOD'S IN THE BOAT

"And when they got into the boat, the wind ceased."

—Matthew 14:32

When I reflect on my accident, I see how the hand of God was at work at every step of my journey. In the dark moments, I could see His light and love. During my recovery, God opened doors for Lori and me to share our faith with doctors, nurses, family, and friends. As we walked out His promise, it strengthened our faith. His plan began to unfold in front of us as we trusted His Word. God didn't cause a distracted (or careless) driver to hit me. But He takes the bad, turns it around, and uses it for good.

Looking back on it and appreciating what happened almost takes my breath away. I see certain things that took place that, in a moment, could have gone in a completely different direction, even with the hospital and the prospect of surgery. The surgeon noticed a hairline correction in the compression of my spine in the X-ray, which caused him to pause before moving forward with back surgery.

Ironically, even though I didn't need any corrective back procedures, today I regularly get approached by people who heard about my accident to say, "I'm getting ready for surgery; would you and Lori pray for me?" So, I can see how this experience opened numerous opportunities for people to find hope in the thought, *God did it for him, and He can do it for me.*

Another thing it did was draw me closer to the Lord. From that day to now, my prayer life has grown stronger. I don't know if it was necessarily recovering from the trauma as much as it was completing the journey. I rejoice whenever I think of the day of my discharge, when the doctor frowned a little bit as he looked at his notes and said, "I'm not going to write you a prescription to take home because you're not taking anything. But if you get home and it starts bothering you, you can call, and we'll get you one."

For the next three weeks, I would take two Tylenol in the morning and two more before bed. Finally, I told Lori, "I'm not going to take any of these tomorrow because I don't know that I need any. I've just been taking them preventively. I'll take the bottle to the office, and if I need one, I'll take one."

That day never came.

DIRECTING OUR STEPS

This shouldn't have surprised me. When Jesus and Peter got into the boat, the waves calmed, and the winds ceased. Something happens when God's in the boat. We can chart our course, agonize over the "what ifs," and make our plans, but God is still in control. As Proverbs 16:9 says, "A man's heart plans his way, but the LORD directs his steps." God's plan is bigger than our storm, and His purposes are greater than our circumstances. God will turn them around for our good and His glory.

This is a principle I find woven throughout Scripture, from Genesis to Revelation. Just look at the formation of the nation of Israel through the twelve sons of Jacob. Jealousy and sibling rivalry led ten of them to toss Joseph into a pit before they decided to sell him to traveling Midianite merchants. Of course, Joseph might not have been the object of scorn if his father hadn't played favorites and given him a multi-colored coat while Joseph bragged about his dreams and of ruling over them all (including their dad) one day.

Then there was the oldest son, Reuben, who slept with Jacob's concubine—a fact Jacob never forgot: "Unstable as water, you shall not excel, because you went up to your father's bed; then you defiled it—He went up to my couch" (Genesis 49:4). And Judah, who impregnated his daughter-in-law after she tricked him because he didn't follow Jewish custom and give her his third son as a husband after the first two died. Jealousy, kidnapping, lying... their list of sins goes on and on. I doubt any of us would have chosen this motley crew as the seeds of a great nation, but God knew what He was doing all along.

> *The way things go in this world proclaims the sovereignty of our God.*

The way things go in this world proclaims the sovereignty of our God. He has the power and authority to transform every aspect of creation to work on behalf of His children. I mentioned this principle being seen orchestrated in the formation of Israel, but we can also see God's hand at work, specifically in the life of Joseph. In hindsight, every struggle, indignity, false accusation, and unjust imprisonment Joseph fought through was part of a bigger plan that he couldn't see in the moment. Yet it all worked for his good.

This is seen in a couple of instances in Genesis. The first takes place in chapter 45 when Joseph's brothers come to him to plead for the return of Benjamin, whom Joseph was holding as a ruse to get his father to come to Egypt. After telling everyone else in the room to leave so he can meet privately with his brothers, Joseph reveals his identity and calms their nerves with these words:

> *"But now, do not therefore be grieved or angry with yourselves because you sold me here; for God sent me before you to preserve life. For these two years, the famine has been in the land, and there are still five years in which there will be neither plowing nor harvesting. And God sent me before you to preserve a posterity for you in the earth and to save your lives by a great deliverance. So now it was* not you who sent me here, but God." —Genesis 45:5–8 *(emphasis added)*

Joseph's words should burn into our spirit: "It was not you who sent me here, but God."

All the indignities and injustice this innocent man faced were part of God's plan. These storms would have reduced many of us to tears, but Joseph pronounced them part of God's plan. The

Lord sent the storms for a higher purpose, just like He does today for His children.

WORKING FOR OUR GOOD

There is a second meeting between Joseph and his brothers back in Israel after Jacob has died and they take him home for burial. To set up the scene, now that their father has passed away, Jacob's sons are afraid their brother Joseph will exact revenge on them for all the injustices he suffered at their hands. So, as they all bowed before him, Joseph reflected on all that had happened to him since that day in the fields with his brothers. It's a laundry list of wrongs:

They threw him in a cistern and sold him to the Ishmaelites for twenty shekels of silver.

They told their father that wild animals had killed him.

The Ishmaelites sold him as a slave in Egypt.

There, he was falsely accused by Potiphar's wife of assaulting her.

Wrongly imprisoned for a crime he didn't commit, he then spent two more years in prison because a man he had helped forgot about him.

He experienced years of suffering and pain because of the actions of his brothers. He endured betrayal and loneliness because of their jealousy.

Genesis 50 describes the scene where—wracked with guilt—the brothers hatch a plan to beg Joseph for forgiveness:

> *When Joseph's brothers saw that their father was dead, they said, "Perhaps Joseph will hate us, and may repay us for all the evil which we did to him." So they sent* messengers

> *to Joseph, saying, "Before your father died he commanded, saying, 'Thus you shall say to Joseph: "I beg you, please forgive the trespass of your brothers and their sin; for they did evil to you."' Now, please, forgive the trespass of the servants of the God of your father."*—vv. 15–17

Joseph's reply appeared a couple of verses later: "Do not be afraid, for am I in the place of God? But as for you, you meant evil against me; but God meant it for good" (vv. 19–20).

In this moment, as Joseph looked back over his life's journey, reflecting on how each setback served as a springboard into his destiny, he could only come to one conclusion: God is in control of all things, and He is orchestrating our circumstances for our benefit. He told his brothers that they meant to hurt him with their evil intentions, but God took all of it and used it for His glory.

This is a foundational biblical principle that is so fundamental and significant that the apostle Paul repeats it in his letter to the church in Rome: "And we know that all things work together for good to those who love God, to those who are the called according to His purpose" (Romans 8:28).

All things. Our God, the Creator of all things, the sustainer of all things, works all things together for good on our behalf.

All things. Our God, the Creator of *all things*, the sustainer of *all things*, works *all things* together for good on our behalf. Appreciating the depth of such a profound truth can transform our Christian journey. Whatever comes into our lives, He is working in it on our behalf whether it is bad accidents, financial setbacks, family problems, or business challenges. Tragedies, troubles, and triumphs—He is working through them all. If we embrace this truth, it will reinforce our faith in the seasons we walk into the unknown. We may not understand everything in the moment, but we know that God is the Conductor of our life's symphony, creating beauty from ashes.

THE FIRE FALLS

That isn't an exaggeration. It came true in my life less than ten months after my accident. I was at our International Executive Council meeting in Cleveland, Tennessee, when the distress call came. Due to my meeting, I missed the first call, thinking our state youth director was calling to fill me in on some details about our children's "Junior Talent" scheduled for the coming weekend at the state campground in South Georgia.

I'll call him back at the break, I thought.

The state campground is a significant parcel of land, with its spacious church building—known as the tabernacle—and other facilities woven into the hearts and history of the South Georgia Church of God family. It opened in 1972 and spans more than 150 acres. It is home to three lakes, dormitories for campers, a gymnasium, a conference center, meeting centers, and a couple dozen homes. Retired ministers and their widows live there. The state office is located there. So are the homes of the state youth director and evangelism director. When Lori and I served as South Georgia youth directors from 2002-2004, our house was on the campground, and my kids fished many nights in the pond out our back door.

It wasn't just the site of major buildings. Our state campground was where many people sensed God calling them to ministry, formed romantic attachments that sometimes led to forever families, or saw divine answers to perplexing dilemmas or physical illnesses delivered in the most miraculous ways. Many noted church leaders had preached at camp meetings or other significant church gatherings over the fifty years of its lifetime. The campground is part of the fabric of churches across Georgia.

When my phone buzzed a second time, I again ignored it because of the business at hand. But when it went off a third time, I told my friend, "I'm sorry, but I'm going to have to step out and take this call. Something's wrong."

I answered my phone in the hallway and asked, "What's going on?"

"It's burning" were the only words the administrative assistant could get out before tears choked off her voice.

"What?" I said. "What's burning?"

"The tabernacle. It's going to be destroyed."

The tabernacle wasn't just an old church building with a few pews for campers. It could seat about two thousand people and was renovated in 2019 to serve our church better. It was the heart of our state. The gathering place that brought us all together. Now, it was a pile of rubble.

At that moment, though, those details didn't matter. I called Lori, and we rushed out of the building to our car for the three-hundred-mile drive to Georgia. As we drove, I asked, "God, how much more can I stand? We are on the verge of our summer camp meeting, and now we have no place to hold worship services."

"God has a plan," Lori said, trying to calm my concerns. "He got us through your accident. I'm confident He will get us through this. We need to find a location for the camp meeting, but you can do that. You've done things like that before. I'm just so thankful no one was injured or worse. It could have been a terrible, deadly situation. What if any of the state youth board members, all ministers with families, had been in there setting up for Junior Talent? We should thank God for His divine protection."

SIGNIFICANT LOSS

To show what this disaster meant, church leaders talked about the fire—determined to be electrical in nature—with sadness in their voices and social media posts. Terry Hart, the overseer for the state of Alabama, talked about being stunned and saddened by the event: "I began my full-time ministry in South Georgia.... I love this place!" he wrote. "It is almost like the passing away of a dear old friend."

General Overseer Tim Hill said: "While we are very thankful that no one was injured, we are heartbroken that a sacred space has been damaged by fire. Our prayers go out to ... the leadership in South Georgia as they deal with this devastating loss."[18]

As I drove, thoughts of the multitude of memories and connections our people had to the tabernacle floated through my mind. As the general overseer said, it was like the passing of an

---

18 "Fire Destroys South Georgia Tabernacle," *Faith News Network*, 20 April 2022, https://www.faithnews.cc/?p=32677.

old friend. Not the bricks and mortar but the events that had unfolded within those walls over fifty years. It's just like a church building. Although it's not the place that makes a congregation, the building where people gather carries a historical significance and symbolic importance to countless lives. If your house burned down and everyone in your family escaped, you would live to see another day but would still mourn the loss.

Before the day ended, I was on the phone numerous times, calling church leaders and pastors to make sure they knew what had happened and to make sure they understood we had a plan. But more importantly, I told them, God had a plan. Then, I turned my attention to finding another facility for our summer camp meeting. The University of Georgia had a conference center in our town; I called my assistant and said, "See if we can get it for these dates so we can use that facility."

"I've already reserved it," Renae quickly replied.

We indeed wound up holding the camp meeting services there that week, but we started the Sunday night camp meeting with a tent service on the foundation, where the tabernacle once stood. We worked feverishly to line up crews to remove all the steel and rubble left by the blaze. Holding the start of camp meeting at the site was an opportunity to collectively mourn our loss, honor our history, and, more importantly, move into our future.

The tabernacle holds a deep history in our church. It was initially built as an open-air building by former General Overseer Ray H. Hughes when he served as the state overseer for Georgia. In addition, countless church leaders, prominent preachers, singers, and musicians had ministered there throughout its fifty-year history. Our speaker that night under the tent was Dr.

Tim Hill, who preached his first camp meeting service there thirty-four years earlier, so the night was filled with nostalgia. But I also wanted people to see this fire wasn't the end of everything; what the enemy meant for evil God would turn into good.

This is a theme that runs throughout the Bible. Even though I've mentioned Lazarus previously, I think the story of him and his sisters is worth repeating. No one could understand why Lazarus had to die. It made no sense. *Why did this happen?* But when you get to the end of the story, Mary and Martha have experienced the love of a compassionate Savior. Through His words, Jesus delivered hope and quickened Martha's faith. Through His tears, Jesus brought peace in the middle of the storm to Mary. At the tomb of Lazarus, He demonstrated power over death, hell, and the grave. What a powerful story!

John recorded the events that followed:

> *Now when He had said these things, He cried with a loud voice, "Lazarus, come forth!" And he who had died came out bound hand and foot with graveclothes, and his face was wrapped with a cloth. Jesus said to them, "Loose him, and let him go." —John 11:43–44*

Jesus raised Lazarus from the dead with three simple words: "Lazarus, come forth!" He was alive! After four days in the grave, Lazarus stood at the mouth of the tomb, resurrected to life.

EXTRAORDINARY SAVIOR

But that isn't where the story ends. Family and friends who had gathered to bring comfort to Mary and Martha during their time of loss became witnesses to the extraordinary events of the day. They saw Jesus's authority and felt His compassion. Most significantly, they witnessed His power. The unexplainable storm opened the door to a harvest: "Then many of the Jews who had come to Mary, and had seen the things Jesus did, believed in Him" (John 11:45).

God used the process of going through the storm as a platform for proclaiming the gospel. Many of the spectators that day became believers. Regardless of the decisions that lead us into a storm, God still works on our behalf. The circumstances we find ourselves in may be the result of bad decisions. Reflecting on my life's journey, most of my problems were caused by poor decisions.

In John 8:44, Jesus called the devil the father of lies. So, whenever we encounter troubles, difficulties, or loss, we can be assured Satan will be there to whisper, "God won't help because you did this to yourself. This is your fault. You created this mess." But regardless of the path that led to the storm, He begins to work the moment we give it to Him.

The death of Jesus on the cross is the ultimate example of God's power at work in all things. History's darkest hour became mankind's greatest moment. Jesus's death on Calvary brings life to all who trust in Him. The disciples could not comprehend how God could use a crucifixion to bring salvation to mankind. But God is at work in all things to fulfill His purpose.

We can't miss the context of this passage. In a fallen world full of suffering and pain, God's primary concern is conforming us into the image of Christ. He works through our storms and difficult circumstances to develop Christlikeness in us.

> *Whatever difficulty, trial, or storm we may face, we have the assurance that it has passed through God's hands of love and grace.*

His ultimate purpose in working things to our good is to make us more like Christ. Whatever difficulty, trial, or storm we may face, we have the assurance that it has passed through God's hands of love and grace.

QUESTIONS FOR DISCUSSION

1) What adversity in your life wound up enabling you to share your faith with someone?

2) How would you describe your prayer life? Is there a way to create a little more time in your daily routine for prayer?

3) As with Joseph, how did something you first saw as a negative turn out to be a positive? How did God work through those circumstances?

4) What significance does a church building, retreat facility, or house have in your life?

Chapter 10

HERE COMES THE SON

"Truly, You are the Son of God."

—Matthew 14:33

When the winds are howling, the waves are crashing, and doubts are building like the crescendo of Beethoven's Fifth Symphony, it is challenging to remain calm and peaceful. I know because of the battles I fought more than once—not just during my stay in the trauma center but afterward when I kept asking the doctor in pleading tones, "You know, this brace doesn't make life easy. I can't drive or bend over. It is miserable to wear during a hot South Georgia summer. When can I get this back brace off?"

Despite the brace, I didn't miss much work. Not because I thought I was indispensable but because moving forward is part of my personality. I wasn't going to let something like this keep me from doing ministry. I couldn't imagine sitting around the house for months. I was going to do what I could to contribute to the tasks at hand.

With my back hurting, at first, I couldn't stay at the office all day. I would come and go, answer calls, complete planning sessions, or meet with our staff before it would be too much. I have to say the team in the South Georgia state office are all champions to me. The state directors handled most of my church appointments during my absence and when I was operating at half-speed. Some pastors who had scheduled me to speak at their churches were kind and understanding and rescheduled appointments without complaint. Looking back on this time, I gained a new appreciation for how supportive everyone was of Lori and me.

Most of all, I thank God for giving me the strength to overcome. First, soon after coming home, He gave me the strength to walk around our neighborhood with Lori. Initially, I could only walk around the block, but we eventually walked three to four miles each evening. God also gave me the energy and the determination to get on my stationary bike. I did that even though I was still wearing my back brace. It wasn't the most pleasurable way to exercise. Still, it helped keep my mind off my circumstances and helped me slowly rebuild my strength. It also helped develop a focus on continually improving and getting better and stronger.

About a month after my accident, I went to see the doctor for follow-up treatment. Before he entered the exam room on that first visit, a nurse met with me for the initial intake screening.

"What medications are you on?" she asked.

"None."

"How would you rate your pain level?"

"Zero," I said with a slight smile.

"So, this happened last year?" she asked.

"No, this happened about four weeks ago."

She shook her head and said, "I've got to get another nurse. Just wait a minute."

When she returned with the second nurse, the latter said, "I've got to meet this guy who was in an accident four weeks ago and has had no surgery, no pain, and no medication."

"It could have killed him!" Lori interjected.

I have realized that not everyone will accept that God still works miracles, that He still does the impossible, and that He is still working in our lives today. But whether the skeptic, doubter, or criticizer believes it or not, He is still a miracle worker.

She was right, but I never thought about it in those terms. From my perspective, it wasn't as big a deal as others may have considered it. It's so remarkable that I occasionally encounter a skeptic who has difficulty believing that God performed a miracle in my life and that He still does the miraculous. I have realized that not everyone will accept that God still works miracles, that He still does the impossible, and that He is still working in our lives today. But whether the skeptic, doubter, or criticizer believes it or not, He is still a miracle worker.

Now, while I wouldn't wish this kind of storm on anyone, sometimes it takes adversity and weakness to help us grasp how much others care for us—and how much God cares for us. I received a more profound revelation of the Lord's character through my storm. His love is more significant than I can comprehend. Regardless of the path life leads us on, His love never fails. His hand is always at work. He is working when we don't see it and when we don't feel it. He is always working in our lives.

TRUSTING GOD

Knowing that the Lord is always working takes a certain amount of faith and trust. I like the observations I found on one site about several biblical characters who trusted God in difficult times. Among the examples, they cited:

Deborah

"Deborah believed and trusted God in a way that can be hard for us to do. God was real and present in her life. She believed that victory was already hers through God. If I had this strong belief that God's hand was in every effort of my day, I would be a lot more content with each day's accomplishments. I wouldn't be so overwhelmed with the busy schedule of my life, but I would believe that I can handle it because God is on my side."

Zechariah and Elizabeth

"Have you been denied something you've longed for for a long time? Maybe it's a lingering health situation that won't go away, a child who rejects your influence, a character weakness you cannot overcome, or a sin that plagues you and your relationships. Zechariah and Elizabeth understand. They also understand how to remain faithful while waiting on God.... What inspires me about Zechariah and Elizabeth is their ability to trust God in the midst of a longing unfulfilled....

"The angel showed up to Zechariah with good news while Zechariah was serving God as a priest. He could have given up on God but decided to keep serving God despite his unfulfilled longing. How do you handle adversity? When we endure adversity for any length of time, it can be easy to lose faith and quickly turn to self-pity and unbelief. This leads us to quit praying and expecting God to move. The story of Zechariah and Elizabeth is about the faithfulness of God and what it means to live by faith."

Moses

"Difficult times can lead us to a point where we feel like our backs are against the wall, and there are minimal options before us to find a way out or a solution to overcome. We are left wondering, 'How did I get myself here?' I felt that when I was hospitalized. 'I can't move, I am in pain. How did I get myself here?'

"I discovered I needed to shift my thinking and see this setback as a set-up for God to move. Moses experienced that same feeling when, after leading Israel out of Egypt, they were stuck between the Red Sea and an angry Egyptian army.... God guided the Israelites to the exact place he wanted them to be, right on the edge of the Red Sea. With the water at their backs, and Pharaoh and the Egyptians bearing down on them, it was only God who could provide a way."[19]

These Bible characters show God's peace is more powerful than our storms. With God, there is a deep, abiding peace in

---

19 "10 Examples of Trusting God in Difficult Times to Inspire You," *Deep Spirituality*, accessed Oct. 26, 20203, https://deepspirituality.com/trusting-god-in-difficult-times/.

the middle of the winds and the waves: "You will keep in perfect peace those whose minds are steadfast because they trust in you" (Isaiah 26:3, NIV). There is perfect peace in Him, regardless of what's happening around us.

REVELATION COMES

The disciples' revelation of Jesus came through the storm. Hours before, they saw Him feed thousands with just a few loaves and fish. In chapter 2, I mentioned how the disciples participated in this miracle. They passed out the food and collected the leftovers. But the miracle didn't reveal Jesus as the Son of God.

Mark's account of the story poignantly addresses this truth, which I pointed out in chapter 4:

> *Then He went up into the boat to them, and the wind ceased. And they were greatly amazed in themselves beyond measure and marveled.* For they had not understood about the loaves, because their heart was hardened. *—Mark 6:51–52 (emphasis added)*

They did not understand what happened with the loaves; they didn't realize who Jesus was—He's the One who can multiply loaves and fishes and walk on water because He is the Son of God.

In Mark 8, Jesus reminded them of the loaves and fish:

> *And Jesus, aware of this, said to them, "Why are you discussing the fact that you have no bread? Do you not yet perceive or understand? Are your hearts hardened? Having eyes, do you not see, and having ears do you not hear? And do you*

not remember? When I broke the five loaves for the five thousand, how many baskets full of broken pieces did you take up?" They said to him, "Twelve." "And the seven for the four thousand, how many baskets full of broken pieces did you take up?" And they said to him, "Seven." And he said to them, "Do you not yet understand?" —vv. 17–21 (ESV)

Jesus and the twelve disciples got in the boat with only one loaf of bread. When Jesus began to speak about the leaven of the Pharisees and the leaven of Herod, the disciples worried about not having any bread. And Jesus asked, "Why are you worried about having no bread?" In other words, they were blinded to the truth that Jesus was the Son of God. They didn't see Jesus as the Answer. They didn't see the spiritual realm and that there was more than the physical world around them. They may have been running low on food, but they were in the boat with Jesus. They would never run out of food when Jesus was in the boat.

Recognizing Jesus for who He is leads us to live a life of faith and worship.

Throughout His earthly ministry, Jesus revealed who He was by His actions. He healed the sick, cast out devils, calmed the stormy seas, multiplied food, and raised the dead. Jesus's actions revealed that He is the Son of God. But for the disciples, His ministry in the storm pulled back the curtain of spiritual blindness and allowed them to see Jesus Christ as the Son of God. Recognizing Jesus for who He is leads us to live a life of faith and worship.

To revisit a story I discussed in chapter 4, on a previous occasion, the disciples frantically woke Jesus at the bottom of the boat. They were afraid because a tempest arose, only to witness Him calm the storm with His words:

> *Then he got into the boat, and his disciples followed him. Suddenly, a furious storm came up on the lake so that the waves swept over the boat. But Jesus was sleeping. The disciples woke him, saying, "Lord, save us! We're going to drown!" He replied, "You of little faith, why are you so afraid?" Then he got up and rebuked the winds and the waves, and it was completely calm. The men were amazed and asked, "What kind of man is this? Even the winds and the waves obey him!"* —Matthew 8:23–27 (NIV)

REVELATION COMES

This time, the disciples understood that Jesus was more than a man, and they declared in Matthew 8:33, "Truly You are the Son of God." The declaration reveals that the disciples had received a revelation that Jesus was indeed God. His actions verified His identity. Only God could walk on water, and only God could command the wind and waves. This is the first time it was shown to the disciples that Jesus is the Son of God. In calling Jesus the "Son of God," the disciples acknowledged His deity; the designation *Son of God* admitted Jesus possessed the exact nature of God.

The revelation of Jesus wasn't found in the miracle. It was discovered in the storm.

> *The revelation of Jesus wasn't found in the miracle. It was discovered in the storm.*

After the wind ceased and the waves calmed, the disciples declared, "Truly you are the Son of God." The revelation of Jesus as divine, as the Son of God, was not seen in the miracle. Mark's version of the story says, "Their hearts were hardened." The miracle didn't crack their stony hearts; it was the storm. Sometimes, we must go through the storm to see who He is. It is the trial that reveals His hand in our circumstances. In the storm, we see His heart of compassion and appreciate how God never leaves our side. In the storm, they saw Jesus.

The day is coming when the Savior will be revealed to all creation as the King of Kings and Lord of Lords. He is described in Revelation as the returning triumphant Ruler. John received a small glimpse of the divinity of Jesus on the sea that day. Later, on the isle of Patmos, He would receive a revelation of who Jesus was, is, and always will be:

> *I saw heaven standing open and there before me was a white horse, whose rider is called Faithful and True. With justice, he judges and wages war. His eyes are like blazing fire, and on his head are many crowns. He has a name written on him that no one knows but he himself. He is dressed in a robe dipped in blood, and his name is the Word of God. The armies of heaven were following him, riding on white horses and*

> *dressed in fine linen, white and clean. Coming out of his mouth is a sharp sword with which to strike down the nations. "He will rule them with an iron scepter." He treads the winepress of the fury of the wrath of God Almighty. On his robe and on his thigh, he has this name written: KING OF KINGS AND LORD OF LORDS. —Revelation 19:11–16 (NIV)*

Jesus is truly the Son of God!

QUESTIONS FOR DISCUSSION

1) Have you ever been through a difficult recovery period when you struggled to regain physical and/or mental capacities? Looking back, what did you gain from this process?

2) How has God shown His love to you during a storm?

3) Of the four biblical figures mentioned in this chapter, whose example struck you as the most significant? Why?

4) Why do you think God wants us to go through situations where we have to depend so heavily on Him?

Chapter 11

OH, COME LET US ADORE HIM!

"Then those who were in the boat came and worshiped Him."

—Matthew 14:33

During the time I lay immobile in the trauma center, I decided that I would not let my problems steal my worship. I was determined to worship God despite the obstacles I faced. I decided to take my focus off my problems and honor the Source of my salvation. My accident would lead me to learn how to worship God in the storm, which came out of nowhere and shook me to the core. Now, I didn't develop this resolve to worship with the expectation of immediate deliverance. I knew this storm had the potential to last for weeks, months, or even longer. But I knew worship was the key to peace and joy in the middle of the howling winds.

> *Maintaining a steady vision of the One who created the world and everything (and everyone) in it will help prevent us from sinking into doom and gloom when adversity strikes*

He is worthy to be lifted on high and exalted. Worship is the one thing we can do when surrounded by the onslaught of a storm. The ups and downs of life have the potential to rapidly shift our attentions from the Lord to our circumstances. But worship can turn our gaze from the storm to the Savior. Praise and worship will change our focus. That may sound like a platitude or cliché, but I assure you that it is not. Maintaining a steady vision of the One who created the world and everything (and everyone) in it will help prevent us from sinking into doom and gloom when adversity strikes.

We don't always feel like praising God in the middle of the storm, especially when we are struggling to keep our heads above water and breathe. When it feels like we are drowning, though, we can do more than survive. A storm can be a place of intimate worship. Our cry for help during a storm can become a declaration of faith to see us through the darkness. In chapter 8, I reviewed how Peter sank into the water when he took his eyes off Jesus. Worship helps to keep us laser-focused on the Savior.

It is vital to cling to the practice of worship because our storms can steal it away. The enemy will attempt to use the turbulence of life to shift our focus and get our eyes to drift from Jesus to our circumstances. But worship is not based on our circumstances, good or bad. Our praise isn't reserved for clear skies and sunny days. We rejoice in every situation. In the good times, we are to praise the Lord. In the bad times, we are to praise the Lord. In everything, give Him praise!

CONTINUAL THANKS

This is what Paul admonished the church in Thessalonica to do: to "give thanks" in every situation: "Rejoice always, pray continually, give thanks in all circumstances; for this is God's will for you in Christ Jesus" (1 Thessalonians 5:16–18, NIV, emphasis added). How is it possible to be thankful in every situation, regardless of how difficult or traumatic the circumstances? Paul answers the question with a two-fold solution: "Rejoice always." Put on the garment of praise for a spirit of heaviness. We walk through our storms with thanks because we walk through them with a heart of worship.

Paul's second key to an attitude of consistent gratitude in the storm is a call to be in continual prayer:

> *Be anxious for nothing, but in everything by prayer and supplication, with thanksgiving, let your requests be made known to God; and the peace of God, which surpasses all understanding, will guard your hearts and minds through Christ Jesus. —Philippians 4:6–7*

Prayer is the key to unlocking the door of peace. In the center of a whirlwind, the peace that surpasses all understanding will only come through Jesus.

This is what David proclaimed in Psalm 34:1–7 (emphasis added):

> *I will bless the LORD at all times;*
> His praise shall continually be in my mouth.
> *My soul shall make its boast in the LORD;*
> *The humble shall hear of it and be glad.*
> *Oh, magnify the LORD with me,*
> *And let us exalt His name together.*
> *I sought the LORD, and He heard me,*
> *And delivered me from all my fears.*
> *They looked to Him and were radiant,*
> *And their faces were not ashamed.*
> *This poor man cried out, and the LORD heard him,*
> *And saved him out of all his troubles.*
> *The angel of the LORD encamps all around those who fear Him,*
> *And delivers them.*

It is easy to praise God when things are going our way. Worship and proclamations of trust in God are easy to express on the mountaintop of victory. The challenge is whether we can praise Him in difficult times when tragedy strikes. What will we do when we are facing a perplexing problem at work, a child who is struggling in school or going a wayward direction, accidents, sickness, a spouse who has an affair or walks away, an addiction, or the death of a loved one? When those storms and trials come, we are to praise Him for who He is at all times. We keep praising God *regardless of what happens.*

As a young Christian, I observed mature believers praise God through tough times, which made an indelible impression on me. I couldn't understand how they could continue to praise God even though it looked like everything was falling apart around them. I gained a powerful spiritual insight from them early in my Christian journey. Praise helps us keep our eyes on God, not our problems. Worship draws our attention to Him and not to ourselves. Through our worship, we learn to trust His heart and hand. I praised and kept my eyes on Jesus instead of my storm.

Praise isn't about how we feel.

When we worship, we focus on who God is. He is our holy, loving, faithful, forgiving, caring, healing, helping heavenly Father. Praise isn't about how we feel. There are times when we don't feel like praising. We are to praise despite what we see or feel. Praise is all about the character of God and the fact that He is worthy of praise. God's character never changes, so our circumstances don't change His character.

FACING THREATS

In 2 Chronicles 20, King Jehoshaphat was facing a serious threat. The Moabites and Ammonites were coming against Judah after the king had returned to seeking God after a near-fatal alliance with Israel's King Ahab. Knowing they were doomed without God's help, Jehoshaphat called the nation to fasting and prayer.

They acknowledged that God was their only hope. Jehoshaphat cried out to God, "For we have no power against this great multitude that is coming against us; nor do we know what to do, but our eyes are upon You" (2 Chronicles 20:12). Jehoshaphat didn't know what to do. His army was no match for the enemy that stood before them. So, he turned his eyes from the overwhelming circumstances and set them upon the Lord.

As Judah marched into battle to face this great multitude, the people had no idea how God was already working on their behalf, but He was:

> *And when he [Jehoshaphat] had consulted with the people, he appointed those who should sing to the LORD, and who should praise the beauty of holiness, as they went out before the army and were saying: "Praise the LORD, for His mercy endures forever." —v. 21*

I hope you caught the significance of what was happening here: the only weapon they raised was the weapon of praise. Over and over, they proclaimed the enduring mercies of God.

The next two verses describe what happened:

> *Now when they began to sing and to praise, the LORD set ambushes against the people of Ammon, Moab, and Mount Seir, who had come against Judah; and they were defeated. For the people of Ammon and Moab stood up against the inhabitants of Mount Seir to utterly kill and destroy them. And when they had made an end of the inhabitants of Seir, they helped to destroy one another. —vv. 22–23*

Their praise was the key to victory. Praise still makes the difference. When troubles come our way, praise Him for who He is and what He will do. Worship becomes our battle cry in the middle of the warfare.

PRAISE CONTINUALLY

I had a church member once who was rather erratic in her worship. One Sunday, she would be on the front row, engaged in worship and seemingly captured by God's Word. She would lift her hands; she would sing loudly and clap even louder. She was enthusiastic and exuberant, no matter who was around her or what anyone else did. If you've been in church for very long, you have likely seen someone just like this woman. She worshiped without concern for what others thought or who was watching.

However, the next Sunday could be a whole other story. She would sit in the back row, never standing, singing, or joining us in prayer. Anyone who had noticed her the previous week would have wondered what in the world had gone wrong. She wasn't just frowning; she refused to worship. She sat there with her arms crossed while wearing a sour, sad countenance. She seemed disinterested in the Word and the service. She reminded me of the old joke about churchgoers who look like they have been baptized in pickle juice.

Finally, I couldn't take it any longer. Approaching her privately, I asked, "What's up with how you participate in worship? One Sunday, you're on fire; the next week, you are completely disengaged and distant in the Lord's presence. Why are you back and forth?"

There are certain pastoral moments you never forget because they are seared into your tapestry of ministry memories. This was one of those moments. She replied, "I refuse to be like the rest of the hypocrites in this church. If I've had a great week, I will come and praise the Lord. But if I've had a bad week, I will not attend church and act as if everything is fine."

After a moment of shock, I told her, "Listen, my life could be in shambles and this past week could have been a disaster that left my world turned upside down. But He is still worthy of my worship! I worship Him despite my circumstances. I will worship Him in the good times and choose to worship Him in the bad times. He is worthy of my worship because of who He is, not what He does for me."

This is one of those stories with a happy ending. Although I was concerned she might react poorly to my advice, get offended, and storm out the door in anger, she remained in the church and became more consistent in her worship. This experience shows how we cannot allow a storm to steal or silence our worship. We must declare as the prophet Habakkuk did:

> *Though the fig tree does not bud*
> *and there are no grapes on the vines,*
> *though the olive crop fails*
> *and the fields produce no food,*
> *though there are no sheep in the pen*
> *and no cattle in the stalls,*
> *yet I will rejoice in the* LORD,
> *I will be joyful in God my Savior.*
> *The Sovereign* LORD *is my strength;*

he makes my feet like the feet of a deer,
he enables me to tread on the heights.
—Habakkuk 3:17–19 (NIV)

REASONS FOR SORROW

Now, Habakkuk had listed numerous reasons for sorrow and despair in the land:

1) There was no fruit on the trees.
2) No crops were growing in the fields.
3) The sheep were scattered.
4) The cattle were gone.
5) Everything was empty.
6) The land had become dry and barren.
7) It seemed that all hope was lost.
8) There was nothing left.
9) The people had no reason for hope or joy.

(Putting everything in a list kind of jars you, doesn't it?)

Yet the prophet declared, "Yet I will rejoice in the Lord!" Despite the circumstances that surrounded him, he chose to rejoice in his salvation. Even in the middle of great pain and suffering, because of the sacrifice of Christ on the cross, we can know joy in the God of our salvation. What a declaration of faith. When everything around us fails and falls apart, we can still have joy and rejoice in God our heavenly Father.

The beauty of trusting in God is that we have in Him a joy and a satisfaction that supersedes the trials of life. God is a treasure who is far better, far greater, and far more wonderful than anything else we could possess. When our journey sends us down a detour to a place of sorrow and suffering, we can choose joy.

It is found in our worship. Habakkuk declared, "I will rejoice"; that's our worship. He then said, "I will be joyful;" that is the result of our worship. The secret to joy in the barren place is worship. When we worship, we replace doubt, fear, and sorrow with unspeakable, indescribable joy. When we focus on Christ, we realize that He is much bigger than our problems. Everything aligns with the proper perspective.

God is a treasure who is far better, far greater, and far more wonderful than anything else we could possess.

So, when life is hard and things are against us, worship. The peace and joy that the storm stole will return to our hearts as we focus on Him. We stand steadfast in Him despite our circumstances. This is why I filled my hospital room in the trauma center with worship. I recounted those figures in Scripture whose weapon was praise: Paul and Silas sang praises in the midnight hour. David worshiped in the desert. Habakkuk rejoiced in a barren land. Daniel prayed in the lion's den. Hezekiah shouted unto God in the face of an overwhelming enemy.

I have seen church members get consumed by financial problems, rebellious children, or stress in their marriage, and instead of praising God and turning to Him for answers, they quit. They stop coming to church, sit at home nursing their wounds, and moan, "I never signed up for this." When I see things like this happen (and I've seen them more than once), I grieve over the loss. Satan has gotten these folks right where he wants them—isolated, depressed, and defeated.

Such sad stories show how we can live our lives consumed by our circumstances, overwhelmed by worry and stress. Or, we can choose to put our focus on Him. He is the One who holds it all in the palm of His hand. God desires our praise. He wants us to surrender our lives completely to Him. He wants us to submit to His presence and experience His power in our lives.

Praise is a choice we make every day. The psalmist wrote,

> *Praise the LORD!*
> *Praise God in His sanctuary;*
> *Praise Him in His mighty firmament!*
> *Praise Him for His mighty acts;*
> *Praise Him according to His excellent greatness!*
> *Praise Him with the sound of the trumpet;*
> *Praise Him with the lute and harp!*
> *Praise Him with the timbrel and dance;*
> *Praise Him with stringed instruments and flutes!*
> *Praise Him with loud cymbals;*
> *Praise Him with clashing cymbals!*
> *Let everything that has breath praise the LORD.*
> *Praise the LORD!* —Psalm 150:1–6

In other words, praise Him in the good times and bad, praise Him in sickness and health, praise Him in wealth and poverty. Let everything that has breath praise the Lord. I repeat: Praise the Lord. As the refrain of that familiar Christmas carol says, "Oh, come let us adore Him."

QUESTIONS FOR DISCUSSION

1) How do you worship God?

2) Have you ever been through difficulties that caused you to stop worshiping Him? What caused you to resume?

3) How do you define rejoicing? Do you know anyone who rejoices even in the midst of deep personal problems? What do you think about that?

4) What is God doing right now in your life that deserves praise?

Chapter 12

THERE'S A MIRACLE WAITING!

"When they had crossed over, they came to the land of Gennesaret. And when the men of that place recognized Him, they sent out into all that surrounding region, brought to Him all who were sick, and begged Him that they might only touch the hem of His garment. And as many as touched it were made perfectly well."

—Matthew 14:34–36

While I have been leading off chapters with snippets from my personal journey during and after my near-fatal bicycle accident, this time I want to save the best for last. Instead, let's focus initially on what happened after the storm on the Sea of Galilee. There is a lesson here for all of us that is still quite relevant for our day and time. In fact, with each passing year, it becomes more relevant.

> *Jesus saves; it is His identity as Savior of the world.*

After Peter's fateful walk on the water, when the boat reached the other shoreline, the people of Gennesaret came out to meet them because they had heard about Jesus. Something always happens when people hear about Jesus. While Scripture doesn't give us the full details, these men who recognized Jesus had gone to the surrounding area to tell people about Him. They must have known Jesus as a healer because the people responded by bringing all their sick to Him. His name means healing, salvation, and miracles. There is power in the very name of Jesus, which literally means "*Yahweh* saves." It's the reason He came to earth in the form of a man: to save and deliver. Jesus saves; it is His identity as Savior of the world. This demonstrates how:

1) *The name of Jesus is mighty to save.*

Our salvation rests on the finished work of Calvary. As the apostle Luke wrote, "Salvation is found in no one else, for there is no other name under heaven given to mankind by which we must be saved" (Acts 4:12, NIV). The truth of Jesus as the only way to heaven is generally rejected by our world. The inter-faith emphasis of modern American culture heralds all faiths as equally valid in their truth. But we who know the forgiving power of Jesus proclaim—even in the face of strong opposition—the same words that He did in John 14:6: "I [Jesus] am the way, the truth, and the life. No one comes to the Father except through Me."

2) *The name of Jesus is mighty to heal.*
The first miracle recorded in Scripture after the ascension was performed in the name of Jesus. Acts records:

> *And fixing his eyes on him [the lame man], with John, Peter said, "Look at us." So he gave them his attention, expecting to receive something from them. Then Peter said, "Silver and gold I do not have, but what I do have I give you:* In the name of Jesus Christ *of Nazareth, rise up and walk." —Acts 3:4–6 (emphasis added)*

The once-lame man leaped to his feet and began praising God. Peter and John were doing what they had witnessed Jesus do. He promised they would receive power when the Holy Spirit came upon them. They were now walking in the promise and authority of His name. When persecution came, they prayed for that kind of authority:

> *"Now, Lord, look on their threats and grant to Your servants that with all boldness they may speak Your word, by stretching out Your hand to heal, and that signs and wonders may be done through the name of Your holy Servant Jesus." And when they had prayed, the place where they were assembled together was shaken; and they were all filled with the Holy Spirit, and they spoke the word of God with boldness. —Acts 4:29–31*

THE SAME POWER

3) *The name of Jesus holds the same power today.*

It is mighty to overcome. As our world becomes more and more evil, we become increasingly aware that our battle is not with "flesh and blood." We are facing demonic attacks and schemes. As Paul wrote to the Ephesians: "For we do not wrestle against flesh and blood, but against principalities, against powers, against the rulers of the darkness of this age, against spiritual hosts of wickedness in the heavenly places" (Ephesians 6:12).

Because we are wrestling with evil, when we face obstacles or accusers, we are not trying to win debates, outwit the opposition, or resort to name-calling. We have spiritual weapons to withstand the enemy's attack:

> *For though we walk in the flesh, we do not war according to the flesh. For the weapons of our warfare are not carnal but mighty in God for pulling down strongholds, casting down arguments and every high thing that exalts itself against the knowledge of God, bringing every thought into captivity to the obedience of Christ. —2 Corinthians 10:3–5*

Because we are wrestling with evil, when we face obstacles or accusers, we are not trying to win debates, outwit the opposition, or resort to name-calling.

As we wage warfare, we should meditate on words like those of English pastor, Edward Perronet, penned in 1780 in his classic hymn, "All Hail the Power of Jesus' Name": "All hail the power of Jesus' name, let angels prostrate fall. Bring forth the royal diadem, and crown Him Lord of all." Amen to that!

This is what the disciples recognized after watching Christ walk on water and calm the storm. Mark's account of the aftermath says when they had crossed over the lake, they landed at Gennesaret and anchored there:

> *As soon as they got out of the boat, people recognized Jesus. They ran throughout that whole region and carried the sick on mats to wherever they heard he was. And wherever he went—into villages, towns, or countryside—they placed the sick in the marketplaces. They begged him to let them touch even the edge of his cloak, and all who touched it were healed. —Mark 6:54–56 (NIV)*

Don't treat this as a ho-hum kind of event. Picture the enormity of what was taking place: People from all over the region were coming to see Jesus. The crowds were chasing after Him and bringing the sick to where "they heard he was." Wherever Jesus went in the region, the sick were healed. Dozens, hundreds, or maybe thousands were healed simply by touching the hem of his cloak as Jesus walked around the shoreline of the Sea of Galilee. There was a miracle waiting on the other side of the storm.

The people of this region had faith in Jesus. It's one thing to be touched by Jesus; it's another level of faith to believe: "If I can just touch His garment, I will be healed." But this is what was happening. The crowds didn't just flock to Jesus; they ran to Him! Those who couldn't get there alone found friends to carry them to Jesus. They *had to get to Jesus* because He is the Miracle Worker!

MIRACLE AFTER MIRACLE

The narrative began with feeding thousands of men, women, and children with a young boy's lunch. As I noted in chapter 2, the disciples were active participants in this incredible miracle. Our story began with a miracle. Moments after this miraculous event, Jesus commanded his disciples to get in the boat, telling them He would meet them on the other side. They soon discovered they had rowed into a storm, but on the other side of the storm, a miracle awaited them.

Do you see the pattern?
Miracle, storm, miracle.

Do you see the pattern? Miracle, storm, miracle. One of the most complex challenges of our Christian walk is waiting during the storm when we need an answer from God. We urgently need Him to intervene in our circumstances. It is difficult to see the possibility of a miracle when we feel overwhelmed by our storm. Storms can rob us of our peace, joy, and hope. They test our faith and challenge our resolve. But if we can hold and simply row a little while longer, we have God's promise of strength and victory. As the prophet Isaiah assures: "Yet those who wait for the LORD will gain new strength; they will mount up with wings like eagles; they will run and not get tired; they will walk and not become weary" (Isaiah 40:31, NASB 1995).

We all get weary occasionally, but God never grows tired. Since He is continually working on our behalf, we need to simply wait on the Lord. God's plan sometimes won't make sense to our human reasoning, but He has a plan. He will see us through to the miracle waiting on the other side of the storm. We can wrestle with God too often and give up too soon. That's because many of us fail to see from God's perspective. We can't view the span of our lives like He can. As Paul said, "For now we see in a mirror, dimly" (1 Corinthians 13:12). Our view is limited, but Jesus knows what every tomorrow holds. We don't know what the future holds, but we know who holds the future: "'For I know the plans I have for you,' declares the LORD, 'plans to prosper you and not to harm you, plans to give you hope and a future'" (Jeremiah 29:11, NIV).

We may not understand why these circumstances enter our lives. We must choose to set aside our plans and trust God. Remember that miracles are not hit or miss. God doesn't just sometimes decide to do a miracle, and sometimes not. The miracle may not come when or how we want it, but we trust God because He is a miracle worker. While we are waiting for the storm to pass, there are faith actions we can take toward the miracle that God has for us.

STEPS TO SOLUTIONS

Regardless of the severity of our storm, we should walk out these seven steps while waiting for God to move:

1) We worship.

Worshiping the Lord has the power to put our circumstances in the proper perspective. Worship puts God at the center of our storm and announces to the world and the devil that we are in the hands of God. It reminds us too. Worship opens the door to our miracle.

2) We listen.

The noise from our storms can be loud. Problems and circumstances will attempt to block out His voice, which sometimes can resemble a faint whisper. Remember how God directed Elijah when he fled into the wilderness, fearing death at the hand of Jezebel:

> *Then He said, "Go out, and stand on the mountain before the LORD." And behold, the LORD passed by, and a great and strong wind tore into the mountains and broke the rocks in pieces before the LORD, but the LORD was not in the wind; and after the wind an earthquake, but the LORD was not in the earthquake; and after the earthquake a fire, but the LORD was not in the fire; and after the fire* a still small voice. —*1 Kings 19:11–12 (emphasis added)*

God's voice is not always loud and overpowering. We must learn to listen to the still, small voice of the Holy Spirit. Be intentional about being quiet before the Lord. Allow the storm to sharpen our listening skills and expect to hear from God.

3) We believe.

The world is screaming no, and our circumstances are crying out the same, but the Lord has already said yes. As Paul put it:

"All the promises of God in Him *are* Yes, and in Him Amen, to the glory of God through us" (2 Corinthians 1:20). God's yes will always overcome every no. That's what a miracle is—the living out of Jesus's instructions to the ruler of the synagogue: "Don't be afraid; just believe" (Mark 5:36, NIV). The devil will fight to steal our faith because he is a thief who comes to kill, steal, and destroy. But we have abundant life in Jesus. We don't get what we deserve; we get what Jesus bought for us on the cross. When Jairus received the news that his daughter had died, Jesus told him to believe. No matter what our circumstances may say, no matter what the devil may say, or what our feelings may try to tell us, we refuse to let doubt and fear direct our steps. Keep believing in God for a miracle that is on the way.

4) We serve.

James 2:26 tells us that "faith without works is dead." While struggling in our storm, we don't just sit around waiting. We act. When Jesus performed His first miracle, John 2 tells us that He and His mother were attending a wedding in Cana of Galilee when the host ran out of wine. Mary asked Jesus to intervene. She was expecting a miracle when she turned to the servants and said, "Whatever He says to you, do it" (v. 5). Whatever the Lord says to do, do it! When we do our part, He will meet us there, doing only what He can do.

5) We stand.

"So, then faith comes by hearing, and hearing by the word of God" (Romans 10:17). The Word of God strengthens our faith because it is unchanging. When the Word is planted in our hearts and minds, it sustains our faith in the storm and helps us to stand. In His key message on the end of the age, Jesus told His disciples, "Heaven and earth will pass away, but My words will by no means pass away" (Matthew 24:35).

Storms will come and go. Circumstances will change. Life will ebb and flow, but Jesus—the living Word of God—will be the same yesterday, today, and forever.

Storms will come and go. Circumstances will change. Life will ebb and flow. But as Hebrews 13:8 says, Jesus—the living Word of God—will be the same yesterday, today, and forever. He is our firm foundation in the storm. Jesus taught the disciples the power of God's Word as our anchor during the floods of life:

> *Therefore, whoever hears these sayings of Mine, and does them, I will liken him to a wise man who built his house on the rock: and the rain descended, the floods came, and the winds blew and beat on that house, and it did not fall, for it was founded on the rock. But everyone who hears these sayings of Mine, and does not do them, will be like a foolish man who built his house on the sand: and the rain descended, the floods came, and the winds blew and beat on that house, and it fell. And great was its fall. —Matthew 7:24–27*

6) We wait.

Faith and patience walk hand in hand. As we wait, we remember this wise advice:

> We *desire that each one of you show the same diligence to the full assurance of hope until the end, that you do not become sluggish, but imitate those who through faith and patience inherit the promises.* —Hebrews 6:11–12

It is our patience and ability to wait that will keep our faith strong until we receive our miracle. Patience will guard us against watching the clock. Let patience have her perfect work. It holds the door of faith open and won't let anything shut it. While we wait, we trust and believe.

7) We expect.

When Jesus healed the boy who was deaf and mute, He told the boy's father, "All things are possible to him who believes" (Mark 9:23). The spirit of expectancy is crucial to victory through our trials. Expecting the impossible opens the door for God's power and allows a supernatural move of God in our lives. Rather than our circumstances, we make God our focus because we expect the miracle that is coming.

NEW GROWTH

Six months after my accident, Lori and I were at the final appointment with my neurosurgeon. He showed us the most recent X-rays of my back on his tablet. As he scrolled through the images, I noticed a bright white in the areas where my back had been broken. Naturally, I asked, "Is that white area where arthritis is in my back?"

His response came quickly.

"No," he said. "It is very uncommon. I've seen it a few times in my years of practice, but only in children. I don't have an explanation; I've never seen it in an adult before. That's new bone growth in your back. I don't believe you will have any lasting effects from your injury. You won't even notice it on a cold rainy day."

Lori immediately declared, "Jesus healed him! The church interceded, and God heard our prayers!"

Never have I been more grateful for a wife who loves God more than me. A slight chill went up my spine, which felt like the Holy Spirit moving through me and saying, *That's right.* Which is why the surgeon's reaction felt like a high five or a fist bump. Throwing up his hands, he said, "Praise the Lord!"

No surgeries, medications, or physical therapy, all because God healed me with His power. He still works miracles! He is still true to His word! Whatever storm we are facing, we must recognize that a miracle is still waiting on the other side of the storm. He makes a way where there seems to be no way. He will always be faithful to His promises. He is a miracle worker—One who still walks on water.

QUESTIONS FOR DISCUSSION

1) Reread Mark 6:54–56. How would you describe what happened in the village of Gennesaret in a modern setting?

2) Why didn't participating in the miracle of the feeding of thousands of people convince the disciples of Jesus's divinity?

3) The author outlines seven steps we can take while waiting for God to move. Which one strikes you as the most significant? Why?

4) What did you think of the surgeon telling Gary that the new bone growth he observed in Gary's back was the first time he had ever seen that take place in an adult? Do you know of anyone who has experienced a similar miracle? Tell others about it.

Always remember...

HE *Still* WALKS ON WATER

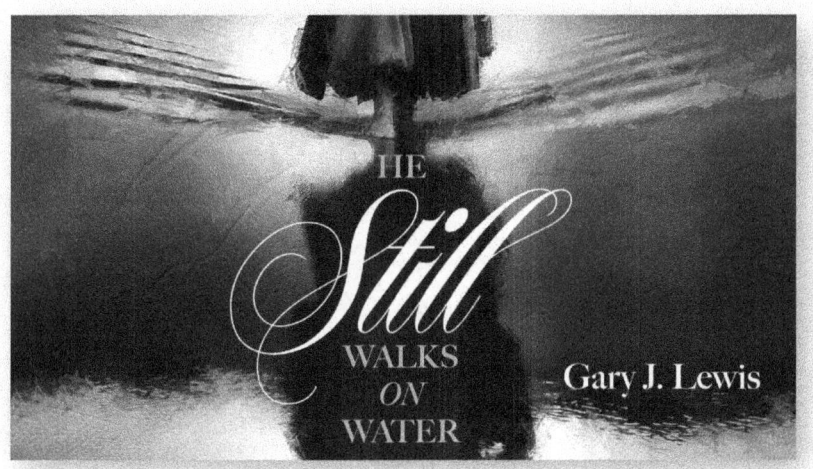

www.ingramcontent.com/pod-product-compliance
Lightning Source LLC
Chambersburg PA
CBHW070538090426
42735CB00013B/3016